RUNIC AND HEROIC POEMS
OF THE OLD TEUTONIC PEOPLES

RUNIC AND HEROIC POEMS
OF THE OLD TEUTONIC PEOPLES

edited by

BRUCE DICKINS

Allen Scholar
Sometime Scholar of Magdalene College

Cambridge:
at the University Press

1915

CAMBRIDGE
UNIVERSITY PRESS

University Printing House, Cambridge CB2 8BS, United Kingdom

Cambridge University Press is part of the University of Cambridge.

It furthers the University's mission by disseminating knowledge in the pursuit of
education, learning and research at the highest international levels of excellence.

www.cambridge.org
Information on this title: www.cambridge.org/9781107636439

First published 1915
First paperback edition 2015

A catalogue record for this publication is available from the British Library

ISBN 978-1-107-63643-9 Paperback

PREFACE

IN preparing this edition I have set before myself a threefold aim; in the first place, to supply a sound, conservative text with all the necessary apparatus, prolegomena, translation, bibliography and notes both critical and exegetical; in the second, to make use of the archæological method which Professor Ridgeway has applied so brilliantly to the study of the Homeric poems; and in the third, to emphasise the essential unity of the old Teutonic languages in 'matter' as in poetic diction. How far it has been accomplished I cannot say: I can at least plead with Marryat's nurse in *Mr Midshipman Easy* that my book is 'such a little one.'

It cannot be claimed that the Runic poems are of any great literary value; they are exactly parallel, indeed, to the old nursery rhyme:

> 'A was an Archer who shot at a frog;
> B was a Butcher who had a big dog.'

But they are of certain interest to the student of social history and of supreme importance in the early history of the English language, a fact most unfortunately neglected in two of the most recent and otherwise the best of English historical grammars.

The Anglo-Saxon poem last appeared in England in 1840; the Norwegian is only available in Vigfússon and

a 3

Powell's *Icelandic Prose Reader* and *Corpus Poeticum
Boreale*; the Icelandic has never before been published in
this country.

The second part of this work contains the extant
fragments of Anglo-Saxon heroic poetry outside *Beowulf*
and *Widsith,* which have been so admirably treated by
Dr Chambers (Cambridge, 1912 and 1914). *Finn* has,
indeed, been edited by Dr Chambers as an appendix to
Beowulf; but my notes were already complete when *Beowulf*
appeared, and as I differ from him on various points—so
much the worse for me in all probability—I have ventured
to include it. It has been a labour of love: for *Finn,*
mutilated and corrupt, is yet the fine flower of Anglo-Saxon
heroic poetry. Full of rapid transitions and real poetic glow,
the fight in Finn's beleaguered hall, lighted by the flash of
swords and echoing with the din of combat, is one of the
most vivid battle-pieces in any language—a theme too often
worn threadbare by dull mechanical prentice-work in later
Anglo-Saxon poetry, when versifying the scriptures became
a devastating industry and the school of Cynewulf antici-
pated by some eight centuries the school of Boyd.

Waldhere has not been edited in English since the
editio princeps of 1860, and Dr W. W. Lawrence's treatment of *Deor* is not very accessible in Volume IX. of
the American journal *Modern Philology.*

The Old High German *Hildebrand* has never before
been edited in English, and I must apologise to experts
for my temerity. It is primarily intended for students of
Anglo-Saxon and Old Norse; but it may, I hope, be useful
to neophytes in German too.

It is now my pleasant duty to thank my many friends in
Cambridge. I have received encouragement and help of the

most substantial kind from the Master, President, Librarian
and Fellows of my own College; from the Disney Professor
of Archæology and the Schröder Professor of German; from
Miss A. C. Paues, of Newnham College, Mr E. C. Quiggin,
of Gonville and Caius College, and Mr E. H. Minns, of
Pembroke College. My friends and fellow students, Miss
N. Kershaw, of St Andrews, and Mr W. F. W. Mortlock,
Scholar of Trinity College, have read part of the MS. From
the staff of the University Library and of the University
Press I have received unfailing courtesy, however much I
have tested their patience. But most of all I have to thank
Mr H. M. Chadwick, Bosworth and Elrington Professor of
Anglo-Saxon, who has rescued me from countless pits which
I had digged for myself. Anyone who has had the good
fortune to work with him will appreciate my debt; no one
else can estimate it. If this volume does anything to
lighten the burdens which he has piled upon himself, I
shall not feel that I have toiled in vain.

B. D.

35 BRUNSWICK SQUARE, W.C.
 October 15th, 1915.

ABBREVIATIONS

Aarb. f. n. O. Aarbøger för nordisk Oldkyndighed og Historie. Kjøbenhavn, 1866–.

Anglia. Zeitschrift für englische Philologie. Halle, 1878–.

Archiv f. n. S. Herrigs Archiv für das Studium der neueren Sprachen und Literaturen. Braunschweig, 1846–.

Arkiv f. n. F. Arkiv för nordisk Filologi. Christiania, 1883–8 ; Lund, 1889–.

B. B. Bonner Beiträge zur Anglistik hrsg. v. M. Trautmann. Bonn, 1898–.

E. St. Englische Studien. Heilbronn, 1877–89 ; Leipzig, 1890–.

Germ. Germania, Vierteljahrsschrift für deutsche Altertumskunde. Stuttgart, 1856–8, Wien, 1859–1892.

M. G. H. Monumenta Germaniae Historica edidit G. H. Pertz ; Scriptorum Tomi xxix. Hannoverae, 1826–.

M. L. N. Modern Language Notes. Baltimore, 1886–.

M. L. R. The Modern Language Review. Cambridge, 1906–.

Mod. Phil. Modern Philology. Chicago, 1903–.

P. B. B. Paul und Braunes Beiträge zur Geschichte der deutschen Sprache und Litteratur. Halle, 1874–.

P. G. (1), (2). Pauls Grundriss der Germanische Philologie. Strassburg, 1891–3, 1896–1909.

P. M. L. A. Publications of the Modern Language Association of America. Baltimore, 1889–.

Tidskrift. Tidskrift for Philologie og Pædagogik. Kjöbenhavn, 1860–.

Z. f. d. A. Haupts Zeitschrift für deutsches Altertum. Leipzig, 1841–53, Berlin, 1856–.

Z. f. d. Ph. Zachers Zeitschrift für deutsche Philologie. Halle, 1869–1908 ; Stuttgart, 1909–.

CONTENTS

THE RUNIC ALPHABET

1. *From the earliest inscriptions*:

ᚠ.ᚢ.ᚦ.ᚨ.ᚱ.ᚲ.ᚷ.ᚹ: ᚺ.ᚾ.ᛁ.ᛃ.ᛈ.ᛉ:

f . u . þ . a . r . k . ӡ . w :   h . n . i . j . ? . p . z . s :

ᛏ. ᛒ.ᛖ.ᛗ.ᛚ. ᛜ. ᛞ.ᛟ::

t . ƀ . e . m . l . ng . ð . o .

2. *Anglo-Saxon.* (*a*) Runic Poem. (*b*) Salzburg Codex.

(*a*) ᚠ.ᚢ.ᚦ.ᚩ.ᚱ.ᚳ.ᚷ.ᚹ: ᚻᚻ.ᚾ.ᛁ. ᛄ.ᛋᛉ. ᚼ.ᛈ. ᛋ:

(*b*) ᚠ.ᚢ.ᚦ.ᚩ.ᚱ.ᚳ.ᚷ.ᚹ: ᚾ .ᛏ.ᛁ.ᛄ ᛋ .ᚼ.ᛈ. ᛋ:

f . u . þ . o . r . c . ӡ . w :   h . n . i . j . i,h . p . z . s .

(*a*) ᛏ.ᛒ.ᛖ.ᛗ.ᛚ.ᛝᛜ.ᛟᚻ.ᛞᚺ: ᚨ.ᚪ.ᚣᚫ.ᛥ [ᛡ.ᛢ.ᛠ.ᛣ]

(*b*) ᛏ. ᛒ.ᛖ ᛗ.ᛗᛚ. ᛝ. ᛟᚻ: ᚨ.ᚪ.ᚩ. ᛥ

t . b . e . m . l . ng . o . d : a . æ . y . *io* . ea . [q . (c) . st . g .]

3. *Scandinavian.* (*a*) Jællinge Stone. (*b*) Runic Poems.

(*a*) ᚠ. ᚢ.ᚦ.ᚭ.ᚱ.ᛦ. ᚼᛏ.ᛁ.ᛐ.ᛋ: ᛏ.ᛒ.ᛚ.ᛘ.ᛧ.

(*b*) ᚠ. ᚢ.ᚦ.ᚭ.ᚱ.ᛦ.ᚼ.ᚼ.ᛁ.ᛐ.ᛁᛁ: ᛐ.ᛒ.ᛚᛦ.ᛘᛧ.

f . u . þ . ǫ . r . k : h . n . i . a . s : t . b . l . m .   ·r·

THE RUNIC POEMS

Building the Runic rhyme, thy fancy roves

SOUTHEY

INTRODUCTION

THE RUNIC ALPHABET

The origin of the Runic alphabet, the native script of the Teutonic peoples, is still a matter of dispute. Isaac Taylor derived it from a Thracian Greek alphabet, Wimmer of Copenhagen from the Latin alphabet; but each of these theories is open to grave objections, and it is perhaps less dangerous to conclude with von Friesen of Upsala that it was taken from a mixture of the two. It is sufficient here to mention that it must have been known to all the Teutonic peoples and that the earliest records go back at least to the fourth century. It was certainly known by the Goths before their conversion; for Wulfila took several of its characters for his Gothic alphabet, and two inscriptions (Pietroassa in Wallachia and Kovel in Volhynia) have been found in lands occupied by the Goths in this period.

In its original form the Runic alphabet consisted of 24 letters, which from the absence of curved or horizontal lines were especially adapted for carving on wood. Testimony is borne by Venantius Fortunatus, whose lines

Barbara fraxineis pingatur runa tabellis
Quodque papyrus agit, virgula plana valet

contain the earliest literary reference to the Runic character; by the Icelandic sagas and by the Anglo-Saxon poem known as the Husband's Message; but from the nature of the case the lance-shaft from Kragehul (Fyn) is almost a solitary

1

survivor of such inscriptions. The alphabet was divided into three sets later styled in Icelandic *Freys ætt, Hagals ætt, Týs ætt,* from their initial letters F, H, T. These names were understood as "Frey's family," etc.; but tripartite division certainly goes back to the original alphabet—it is found on the sixth century bracteate from Vadstena, Sweden—and it is more probable that *ætt* is derived from *átta,* "eight," and so originally meant "octave." Each letter, moreover, occupied a definite position; for in Codex Sangallensis 270 are to be found several varieties of Runic cypher—*Isruna, Lagoruna, Hahalruna, Stofruna*—the solution of which demands a knowledge of the exact position of each letter in the alphabet. Thus in the Latin *Corui,* the example given, the sixth letter of the first series is C, the eighth of the third O, the fifth of the first R, the second of the first U, the third of the second I[1]. A cypher similar in type to the *Hahalruna* of the St Gall MS., but adapted to the Scandinavian alphabet of the Viking Age, is to be found in the grave-chamber at Maeshowe (Orkney), and there are traces of similar characters, now for the most part illegible, in Hackness Church near Scarborough.

Among the earliest inscriptions from the North of Europe are those found in the bog-deposits of Nydam and Torsbjærg in Slesvig, Vi and Kragehul in Fyn, etc., which range in date from the third or fourth to the sixth century. They are written in a language which may be regarded as the common ancestor of English and Scandinavian; it still preserves the full inflections and is thus more primitive than the Gothic of Wulfila. The contemporary inscription from the Golden Horn of Gallehus (Jutland) may be quoted as an illustration, *Ek Hlewaʒastiz Holtingaz horna tawido.* (I Hlewagastiz Holtingaz made the horn.)

---

[1] These cryptograms are possibly to be attributed to Hrabanus Maurus, Abbot of Fulda (822–856), who is known to have been interested in the Runic alphabet; cf. the *Abecedarium Nordmannicum,* p. 34 and his treatise *De Inventione Linguarum* (Migne cxii. 1582). *Coruus* is the Latin equivalent of Hraban (ON. *Hrafn*) and medieval scholars were fond of Latinizing their Teutonic names, e.g. Hrotsvith (*Clamor validus*), Aldhelm (*Vetus galea*).

To the same period belong a brooch found at Charnay in Burgundy, and probably also an inscribed spear-head from Müncheberg (Brandenburg), together with two or three smaller objects found in the north of Germany. In Germany, however, inscriptions of this character are quite rare and mostly unintelligible, the latest belonging probably to the eighth century.

There can be no reasonable doubt that the alphabet was introduced into England by the Saxon invaders in the fifth century, though the inscriptions dating from the first two centuries after the invasion are very few and fragmentary. Among them we may especially note those on a gold coin of unknown provenance in imitation of a *solidus* of Honorius and a scabbard-mount from Chessell Down in Wight. These are connected by the forms of the letters with inscribed objects from Kragehul and Lindholm (Skåne), which date in all probability from the early part of the sixth century, though the English inscriptions may be somewhat later. Runic legends also occur on a number of silver coins, some of them bearing the names *Æþil(i)ræd* (doubtless the Mercian king Aethelred, 675–704), or *Pada*, identified by some with Peada, brother of Aethelred, by others, and more probably, with his father Penda (d. 655). Runes are also found on a number of other small objects of metal or bone, the most interesting of which is the Franks Casket, generally believed to date from about 700.

The gradual disuse of the Runic alphabet is well illustrated by coins of the eighth and ninth centuries. The last king whose name appears in Runic characters is Beonna of East Anglia (c. 750), and even on this coin a Roman O is found. On coins of subsequent kings we only meet with an occasional Runic letter, usually L. In the names of moneyers, however, the Runic letters seem to have persisted somewhat longer; for there are a number of coins issued by Eanred of Northumbria (809–841 ?), on which two of his moneyers signed their names in Runic characters.

Of memorial stones there are in existence nearly a

score (principally in the North of England) bearing inscriptions in the English Runic character. The most notable
of these are the elaborately carved crosses at Ruthwell
(Dumfries)—with verses abridged from the *Dream of the
Cross*—and Bewcastle (Cumberland), the grave slab with
inscriptions both in Roman uncials and Runic characters
from Falstone (Northumberland), and the three stones from
Thornhill (Yorks.).   Cf. Thornhill III. *Gilsuiþ arærde æfter
Berhtsuiþe becun on bergi. Gebiddaþ þær saule.* (Gilswith
erected to the memory of Berhtswith a monument on the
tomb.   Pray for her soul.)   The earliest date probably
from the seventh century; while the latest contain forms
which point to about the middle of the ninth.   There
seems no reason, however, for supposing that for this
purpose the English Runic alphabet remained longer in
use than for coins.   At all events there is no evidence
that it survived the great Danish invasion of 866, which
swept away the upper classes in the greater part of
Northern England.   After this time we find only MS. Runic
alphabets, doubtless preserved as antiquarian curiosities,
except for the letters *wyn* and *þorn*, which had been
adopted into the Anglo-Saxon book-hand, and *eðel, dæg*
and *man*, which were occasionally used as shorthand in
the MSS.

From the sixth century, however, the alphabet had
developed on totally different lines in Scandinavia and
England.   To the original 24 letters the English eventually
added six, *æsc, ac, yr, ear, calc, gar,* if not a seventh *ior*.
The Scandinavian alphabet, on the other hand, continually
reduced the number of letters, until by the ninth century
no more than sixteen were left.   How incapable they were
of representing the sounds of the language can be seen from
the greater Jællinge stone set up by Harold Bluetooth, king
of Denmark (c. 940–986):

*Haraltr kunukR baþ kaurua kubl þansi aft Kurm faþur sin auk
aft þaurui muþur sina, sa Haraltr ias sąr uan Tanmaurk ala auk
Nuruiak auk Tani karþa kristną.*

(King Harold ordered this monument to be made to the

memory of Gorm his father and Thyre his mother, that Harold who conquered all Denmark and Norway and christianised the Danes.)

From the beginning of the eleventh century, however, the alphabet was supplemented by the so-called "dotted runes" (*stunginn k, i, t, b = g, e, d, p*).

The later Runic alphabet was known in Denmark, Sweden, Norway, Iceland, Greenland, the Faroes, the Orkneys, Man and England, in every part of the Scandinavian world; even in the South of Russia an inscription has been found. In Denmark there are something less than 200 inscriptions, few of which are later than 1150; in Sweden there are nearer 2000, some of which can scarcely be earlier than the fifteenth century. Scandinavian also in language and in character are the inscriptions from the Orkneys and Man. In England, too, there are a few relics of the Danish conquest, such as the sculptured stone in the library at St Paul's (c. 1030) and the *þorfastr* comb from Lincoln in the British Museum[1].

In Norway and Iceland, however, the Runic alphabet is never found on monumental stones of the Viking Age, though it was used commonly enough for other purposes. The later Norwegian inscriptions date from the period 1050–1350, the Icelandic are not earlier than the thirteenth century. Generally speaking we may say that the Runic alphabet, always connected more or less with magical practices, fell under the suspicion of witchcraft in the Scandinavian countries and perished in the great outburst of superstitious terror which followed the establishment of the reformed religion, though there is some little evidence to show that in Sweden it lingered on into the nineteenth century[2].

---

[1] The Bridekirk font (Cumberland) bears a twelfth century English inscription in the Scandinavian Runic characters of that time with a few additional letters borrowed from the Anglo-Saxon book-hand.

[2] There is not much evidence for the magic use of runes in this country. Bede (*H.E.* IV. 22) tells the story of a Northumbrian noble captive to the Mercians at the battle of the Trent (679), whose chains were mysteriously loosened, whenever his brother, who thought him dead, celebrated masses for the repose of his soul. His gaoler in ignorance asked him whether he had

THE ANGLO-SAXON RUNIC POEM.

The Anglo-Saxon Runic Poem is taken from the Cottonian MS. Otho B x, which perished in the fire of 1731. It had, however, been printed by Hickes in his *Linguarum Veterum Septentrionalium Thesaurus*, I. 135 (London, 1705), from which the present text is derived. It consists of short stanzas, 29 in all, of two to five lines each, at the beginning of which stand the Runic characters described, preceded by their equivalents in ordinary script and followed by their names. It has been suggested, however, that in Otho B x, as in the Norwegian poems, the Runic characters alone were found, the names being added from some other MSS. At any rate Hempl, *Mod. Phil.* I. 135 ff., has shown that the variant runes, etc., were taken from Domitian A IX, and some such theory is needed to account for the frequent discrepancy between the stanzas and the names which they describe. This may be due in part to the lateness of the MS., which from linguistic criteria can scarcely have been earlier than the eleventh century, e.g. v. 37, *underwreþyd* for *-od* (*-ed*), and vv. 32, 91, ðon, ðonn for ðonne. The poem must, however, be far earlier, pre-Alfredian at least (with traces perhaps of an original from which the Scandinavian poems are likewise derived); for there is not a single occurrence of the definite article, ðone in v. 70 being demonstrative. The versification is moreover quite correct. Cf. Brandl, *Grundriss der germanischen Philologie₂*, II. 964.

THE NORWEGIAN RUNIC POEM.

The Norwegian Runic poem was first printed (in Runic characters) by Olaus Wormius, *Danica Literatura Antiquissima*, p. 105 (Amsterodamiae, 1636), from a law MS. in

litteras solutorias, de qualibus fabulae ferunt, concealed about his person. These *litterae solutoriae* are doubtless to be compared with Hávamál, CL :

> þat kannk et fjórþa ef mér fyrþar bera
> bǫnd at boglimum
> Svá ek gel at ek ganga má
> sprettr af fǫtum fjǫturr
> en af hǫndum hafi.

the University Library at Copenhagen, which perished in
the fire of 1728. This version was used by Vigfússon and
Powell in their *Icelandic Prose Reader* (Oxford, 1879) and
Corpus Poeticum Boreale (Oxford, 1883), where the textual
difficulties are dealt with in a very arbitrary fashion.

The MSS. had, however, been copied later in the seventeenth century by Arni Magnússon and Jón Eggertson,
whose transcripts, far more accurate than Worm's, exist at
Copenhagen and Stockholm. It was on these that Kålund
based his text in the first critical edition, *Småstykker*
(København, 1884–91), pp. 1 ff., 100 ff., in which are in-
corporated valuable suggestions by Sophus Bugge and
B. M. Ólsen. Kålund added the names of the Runic letters,
but printed the texts in their original orthography. In this
edition, however, it has been thought more satisfactory
to adopt the normalised Old Norwegian spelling used in
the German translation of Wimmer's great work, *Die Runenschrift*, pp. 273–80 (Berlin, 1887).

The poem, which has certain affinities to the Anglo-
Saxon, is ascribed to a Norwegian author of the end of the
thirteenth century; *ræið* and *rossom* alliterate, which would
be impossible with the Icelandic forms *reið* and *hrossum*.
It is composed in six-syllabled couplets, each of which contains two semi-detached statements of a gnomic character;
the first line, which has two alliterating words, is connected
by end-rhyme (except in the case of 15) and enjambement
with the second which has none.

THE ICELANDIC RUNIC POEM.

The Icelandic Runic Poem, which is supposed to date
from the fifteenth century, is somewhat more elaborate than
its Norwegian prototype. It consists of sixteen short stanzas
dealing in succession with the letter names of the Scandinavian Runic alphabet. In each of these stanzas are
contained three *kenningar*—the elaborate periphrases which
bulked so large in the technique of the Icelandic skaldic
poems. The first and second lines are connected by

alliteration, the third has two alliterating syllables of its own.

The Icelandic Runic alphabet contained several more letters at this time; but only the sixteen current in the Viking Age are treated here. This is perhaps natural if the poem is derived from a much earlier original, though it does not seem that the later dotted U, K, I, T, B, introduced to represent O, G, E, D, P (with the possible exception of P, *plastr*), had names of their own. They were simply called *stunginn Íss, stunginn Týr*, etc.—dotted I, dotted T, etc.

The poem is taken from four MSS. in the Arnamagnaean Library at Copenhagen.

1. AM. 687, 4to, parchment of the fifteenth century and containing the Runic characters, but not the names.
2. AM. 461, 12mo, parchment of the sixteenth century, with names only.
3. AM. 749, 4to, paper of the seventeenth century, with names and letters in alphabetical order, followed by "dotted runes."
4. AM. 413, folio, pp. 130–5, 140 ff., from parchments of the sixteenth century copied in Jón Ólafsson of Grunnavík's MS. *Runologia* (1732–52),
   (*a*) with names and letters in alphabetical order,
   (*b*) with names and letters in Runic order except that *lǫgr* precedes *maðr*.

Cf. Kålund, *Småstykker*, pp. 16 ff.; Wimmer, *Die Runenschrift*, pp. 281 ff.

BIBLIOGRAPHY OF THE RUNIC POEMS.

The Runic Alphabet.

The extensive literature of the last thirty or forty years will be found noted in the *Jahresbericht für germanische Philologie* (Leipzig, 1879–1914); only the more important books and articles can be mentioned here.

Liljegren, J. G. *Run-Lära.* Stockholm. 1832.

Liliencron, R. von and Müllenhoff, K. *Zur Runenlehre (Allgem. Monatsschrift,* pp. 169 ff., 310 ff.). Kiel. 1852.

Stephens, G. *The Old Northern Runic Monuments of Scandinavia and England.* 4 vols. London and Kjøbenhavn. 1866–1901.

—— *Handbook of the Old Northern Runic Monuments.* L. & K. 1884.

—— *The Runes, whence came they?* L. & K. 1892.

Taylor, I. *Greeks and Goths.* London. 1879.

Burg, F. *Die älteren nordischen Runeninschriften.* Berlin. 1885.

Wimmer, L. F. W. *Die Runenschrift.* Berlin. 1887.

—— *De tyske Runemindesmærker (Aarb. f. n. O.* 1894. pp. 1 ff.).

Henning, R. *Die deutschen Runendenkmäler.* Strassburg. 1889.

Bugge, S. *Norges Indskrifter med de ældre Runer.* Christiania. 1891–1903.

—— *Der Runenstein von Rök.* Stockholm. 1910.

—— *Runinskriftens Oprindelse.* Christiania. 1905–1913.

Sievers, E. *Runen und Runeninschriften (P. G.,* I. 238 ff.). Strassburg. 1891.

Friesen, O. von. *Om Runskriftens Härkomst.* Uppsala. 1904.

Paues, A. C. *Runes and Manuscripts (Camb. Hist. Eng. Lit.* I. 7 ff.). Cambridge. 1907.

Neckel, G. *Zur Einführung in die Runenforschung (Germanisch-Romanische Monatsschrift,* I. pp. 7 ff., 81 ff.). Heidelberg, 1909.

Noreen, A. *Altisländische und altnorwegische Grammatik₃.* Halle. 1903.

Liljegren, J. G. *Run-Urkunde.* Stockholm. 1833.

Thorsen, P. G. *De danske Runemindesmærker.* 3 vols. Kjøbenhavn. 1864–1880.

—— *Codex Runicus.* Kjøbenhavn. 1877.

Wimmer, L. F. W. *De danske Runemindesmærker.* 4 vols. Kjøbenhavn. 1895–1905.

do. *haandudgave ved Lis Jakobsen.* København. 1914.

Bugge, S. *Norges Indskrifter med de yngre Runer.* Christiania. 1902, 1906.

10 Bibliography

Of the Swedish inscriptions now in course of publication by the *Kongl. Vitterhets Historie och Antiqvitets Akademi* the following have appeared :

Söderborg, S. and Brate, E. *Ölands Runinskrifter.* Stockholm. 1900–1906.

Brate, E. *Östergötlands Runinskrifter,* I. Stockholm. 1911.

Kålund, K. *Islands Fortidslævninger (Aarb. f. n. O.* 1882. pp. 57 ff.).

Ólsen, B. M. *Runerne i den oldislandske Literatur.* København. 1883.

Jónsson, F. *Runerne i den danske-islandske Digtning og Litteratur (Aarb. f. n. O.* 1910. pp. 283 ff.).

Farrer, J. *Notice of Runic Inscriptions discovered during recent excavations in the Orkneys.* Printed for private circulation. 1862.

Kermode, P. M. C. *Manx Crosses.* London. 1907.

Sweet, H. *The Oldest English Texts.* E.E.T.S. London. 1885.

Vietor, W. *Die northumbrischen Runensteine.* Marburg. 1898.

Chadwick, H. M. *Early Inscriptions from the North of England* (Yorkshire Dialect Society, Part III). Bradford. 1901.

Napier, A. S. *The Franks Casket* (Furnivall Misc., pp. 362 ff.). Oxford. 1901.

THE ANGLO-SAXON RUNIC POEM.

Hickes, G. *Linguarum Veterum Septentrionalium Thesaurus,* I. 135. London. 1705.

Grimm, W. K. *Über deutsche Runen,* pp. 217 ff. Göttingen. 1821.

Kemble, J. M. *Archaeologia,* XXVIII. 339 ff. London. 1840.

Ettmüller, L. *Engla and Seaxna scôpas and bôceras,* pp. 268 ff. Quedlinburg. 1850.

Zacher, J. *Das gotische Alphabet Vulfilas u. d. Runenalphabet.* Leipzig, 1855.

Grein, C. W. M. *Bibliothek der angelsächsischen Poesie,* II. 354 ff. Cassel. 1858.

—— *Germ.* x. 428.

Rieger, M. *Alt- und angelsächsisches Lesebuch,* pp. 136 ff. Giessen. 1861.

Botkine, L. *La Chanson des Runes.* Havre. 1879.

Wülker, R. P. *Kleinere ags. Dichtungen,* pp. 37 ff. Halle. 1882.

Grein-Wülker. *Bibliothek der ags. Poesie,* I. 331 ff. Kassel. 1883.

Wülker, R. P. *Grundriss z. Geschichte d. ags. Litteratur.* Leipzig. 1885.

Meyer, R. M. *Die altgermanische Poesie,* pp. 21 ff. Berlin. 1889.

Brooke, Stopford A. *History of Early English Literature,* I. 342 ff. London. 1892.

v. Grienberger, Th. *Die germanischen Runennamen* (*P.B.B.*, XXI. 185 ff.). Halle. 1896.

—— *Die ags. Runenreihen* (*Arkiv f. n. F.* XV. 1 ff.). Lund. 1899.

Chadwick, H. M. *Anzeiger f. indogermanische Sprach- und Altertumskunde*, IX. 60–63. Strassburg. 1898.

Kluge, F. *Angelsächsisches Lesebuch* (3), pp. 152 ff. Halle. 1902.

Hempl, G. *Hickes' additions to the Runic Poem.* (*Mod. Phil.*, I. 135 ff.) Chicago. 1903.

Meyer, R. M. *Die altgermanische Runengedichte* (*P.B.B.* XXXII. 67 ff.). Halle. 1907.

Brandl, A. *Geschichte d. ae. Literatur* (Paul's *Grundriss d. germanischen Philologie* (ed. 2), II. 964 ff.). Strassburg. 1908.

THE SCANDINAVIAN RUNIC POEMS.

O. Wormius. *Danica Literatura Antiquissima*, pp. 105 ff. Amsterodamiae. 1636.

W. K. Grimm. *Über deutsche Runen*, pp. 246 ff. Göttingen. 1821.

P. A. Munch. *Kortfattet Fremstilling af den nordiske Runenskrift*, pp. 7 ff. Christiania. 1848.

G. Vigfússon and F. Y. Powell. *Icelandic Prose Reader*, pp. 440 ff. Oxford, 1879.

—— *Corpus Poeticum Boreale*, II. 369 ff. Oxford. 1883.

Kr. Kålund. *Småstykker*, pp. 1 ff., 100 ff. København. 1884–91.

L. F. A. Wimmer. *Die Runenschrift*, pp. 273 ff. Berlin. 1887.

F. Holthausen. *Altisländisches Lesebuch*, p. 93. Weimar. 1896.

THE ANGLO-SAXON RUNIC POEM

1   Feoh byþ frofur   fira gehwylcum ;
    sceal ðeah manna gehwylc   miclun hyt dælan
    gif he wile for drihtne   domes hleotan.

4   Ur byþ anmod   *ond* oferhyrned,
    felafrecne deor,   feohteþ mid hornum
    mære morstapa;   *þæt* is modig wuht.

7   Ðorn byþ ðearle scearp;   ðegna gehwylcum
    anfeng ys yfyl,   ungemetum reþe
    manna gehwylcum,   ðe him mid resteð.

10 Os byþ ordfruma   ælcre spræce,
    wisdomes wraþu   ond witena frofur
    and eorla gehwam   eadnys ond tohiht.

1. *Feoh.* Cf. AS. *fech*, Gothic *fe* from Salzburg Codex 140, a late copy of a Northumbrian text which there is some evidence for connecting with Alcuin. Cf. Chadwick, *Studies in Old English* (Camb. Phil. Soc. 1899, p. 117). Cf. Wimmer, *die Runenschrift*, p. 85.

4. *Ur* (Salz. AS. *ur*, Goth. *uraz*). Cf. ON. *úrr*, OHG. *urohso*; bos taurus primigenius, the aurochs or buffalo, the gigantic wild ox described by Caesar, *B.G.* vi. 28, as inhabiting the Hercynian forest :

> *Tertium est genus eorum qui uri appellantur. Hi sunt magnitudine paulo infra elephantos, specie et colore et figura tauri. Magna vis eorum est et magna velocitas, neque homini neque ferae quam conspexerunt parcunt.... Amplitudo cornuum et figura et species multum a nostrorum boum differt.*

It is to be distinguished from the bison (e.g. Seneca, *Phaedra*, v. 68 ;

> *Tibi dant variae pectora tigres,*
> *Tibi villosi terga bisontes,*
> *Latibus feri cornibus uri,*

and Pliny, *Nat. Hist.* viii. 15) with which it was confused in medieval Germany, cf. Albertus Magnus, *De Animalibus*, xxii. 2.

"Its remains occur abundantly in the later Plistocene deposits of Britain, those from the brick-earths of Ilford, in Essex, being remarkable for their fine state of preservation and showing the enormous dimensions attained by this magnificent animal" (Lydekker, *Wild Oxen*, p. 11, London, 1898). In Western Europe, however, it was still found in the Middle Ages ; in the sixth century it was hunted in the Vosges (Gregory of Tours, x. 10, Venantius Fortunatus, *Misc.* vii. 4. 19 ; cf. Nibelungenlied, str. 880), and doubtless in other thickly wooded regions, but was extinct by the end of the period. In Poland alone it persisted somewhat longer in the forest of Jakozowska (described and illustrated by von Herberstein, *Rerum Moscovitarum Commentarii*, Antwerp, 1557), where the last was killed in 1627. Cf. Lydekker, *The Ox and its Kindred*, pp. 37–67, pl. ii. iii. (London, 1912).

The horns of the aurochs, occasionally 6½ feet in length with a capacity of well nigh a gallon, were much prized as drinking vessels in medieval Europe, cf. Egilssaga, c. xliv. 3, Saxo, Bk vi. (Holder, p. 168) ; and the poet, who is scarcely likely to have seen an aurochs in the flesh, may have used one brought to England from the continent.

THE ANGLO-SAXON RUNIC POEM

F. (wealth) is a comfort to all men; yet must every man bestow it freely, if he wish to gain honour in the sight of the Lord.

U. (the aurochs) is proud and has great horns; it is a very savage beast and fights with its horns; a great ranger of the moors, it is a creature of mettle.

Þ. (the thorn) is exceedingly sharp, an evil thing for any knight to touch, uncommonly severe on all who sit among them.

O. (?   ) is the source of all language, a pillar of wisdom and a comfort to wise men, a blessing and a joy to every knight.

Hence *oferhyrned*, "with great horns," *ofer* being intensive as in vv. 29, 71, *oferceald*, *oferleof*.

7. *þorn*, so in all AS. Runic alphabets and in most of the OHG. derivatives (cf. v. Grienberger, *Ark. f. n. F.* xv. p. 1 ff.). þ was adopted into the AS. book-hand and persisted throughout the ME. period, the last trace of it surviving in the archaistic *ye* (for *the*).

The Scandinavian alphabets, however, have *þurs* (cf. AS. *þyrs*, a giant), and the Salzburg Codex Gothic *thyth*, which have no connection with each other or with AS. *þorn*.

10. *Os* (Salzb. AS. *os*) < * *ansuz*, a god (cf. Jordanes, c. xiii., *Gothi...proceres suos, quorum quasi fortuna vincebant, non puros homines, sed Ansis, id est semideos, vocaverunt*, and the ON. *áss*), the name of A in the original alphabet. Cf. *A(n)suʒisalas* of the Kragehul lance-shaft. But original *a* seldom remained in AS., and the character became the English Runic letter for *æ* (*æsc*). Accordingly a ligature of A and N was invented to express the *ō*, which arose from *-an-* followed by þ or *s*. Later, when the name of the original O letter had become *œðel*, *os* was used for *o* in all cases, whatever might have been their origin.

Os is a common element in AS. personal names, e.g. Oswald, Oswine, etc. ; cf. *A(n)suʒisalas* above, and its Gen. pl. *esa* used in the charm *wið færstice* (G.-W. i. 318)

> *gif hit wære esa gescot oððe hit wære ylfa gescot*
> *oððe hit wære hægtessan gescot, nu ic willan þin helpan.*

Its precise meaning here is perhaps open to question, though the collocation *æsir ok alfar* is common in ON. mythological poetry.

In the Icelandic poem *óss*, which likewise represents original * *ansuz*, = Othin, and it is just possible that this stanza refers to some such episode as that described in *Gylfaginning*, c. ix. ; *þá er þeir gengu með sævarströndu Borssynir* (Óðinn, Vili and Vé), *fundu þeir tré tvau ok tóku upp tréin ok skǫpuðu af menn; gaf inn fyrsti ond ok líf, annarr vit ok hræring, III ásjónu, mál ok heyru ok sjón*. But it is not very likely that the origin of human speech would be attributed to a heathen divinity, and on the whole it is preferable to assume that the subject of the stanza is the Latin *os*, mouth, which would be equally appropriate.

13 Rad byþ on recyde   rinca gehwylcum
   sefte ond swiþhwæt,   ðamðe sitteþ on ufan
   meare mægenheardum   ofer milpaþas.

16 Cen byþ cwicera gehwam,   cuþ on fyre
   blac ond beorhtlic,   byrneþ oftust
   ðær hi æþelingas   inne restaþ.

19 Gyfu gumena byþ   gleng and herenys,
   wraþu *and* wyrþscype   *and* wræcna gehwam
   ar and ætwist,   ðe byþ oþra leas.

22 Wenne bruceþ,   ðe can weana lyt
   sares and sorge   and him sylfa hæfþ
   blæd *and* blysse   and eac byrga geniht.

25 Hægl byþ hwitust corna;   hwyrft hit of heofones lyfte,
   wealcaþ hit windes scura;   weorþeþ hit to wætere
   syððan.

27 Nyd byþ nearu on breostan;   weorþeþ hi þeah oft
   niþa bearnum
   to helpe and to hæle gehwæþre,   gif hi his
   hlystaþ æror.

29 Is byþ oferceald,   ungemetum slidor,
   glisnaþ glæshluttur   gimmum gelicust,
   flor forste geworu*h*t,   fæger ansyne.

22. Hickes, *wen ne.*   31. *geworulit.*

13. *Rad* (Salz. AS. *rada*, Goth. *reda*), as in other alphabets. It is most satisfactory on the whole to take *rad* as "riding," cf. *ræið*, *reið* of the Norwegian and Icelandic poems.

"Riding seems an easy thing to every warrior while he is indoors, and a very courageous thing to him who traverses the high-roads on the back of a stout horse," though it is doubtful whether *byþ* can mean "seems," and neither *hwæt* nor any of its compounds are used of things.

Professor Chadwick has, however, suggested to me that the proper name of this letter is *rada* of the Salzburg Codex, corresponding to the ON. *reiði*, "tackle (of a ship)," "harness," hence "equipment" generally. Here it would be used in a double sense, in the first half as "furniture" (cf. ON. *reiðustól*, "easy-chair," AS. *rædesceamu*), in the second as "harness."

16. *Cen* (Salzburg AS. *cen*, Goth. *chozma*?) found only as the name of the Runic letter C. Cf. OHG. *kien*, *kēn*; pinus, fax, taeda, "resinous pine-wood," hence "torch." Like the ON. K (*kaun*), it is descended from the K (<) of the earliest inscriptions. From the sixth century, at least, English and Scandinavian developed on independent lines, the point of divergence being marked by the lance-shaft from Kragehul (Fyn) and the snake from Lindholm (Skåne), which has the same intermediate form of K (ᛣ) as the earliest of English inscriptions, the SKANOMODU coin and the scabbard-mount from Chessell Down. But in AS. *c* and *g* became palatal before front vowels, and the original letters were used for this sound, new

R. (?) seems easy to every warrior while he is indoors and very courageous to him who traverses the high-roads on the back of a stout horse.

C. (the torch) is known to every living man by its pale, bright flame; it always burns where princes sit within.

G. (generosity) brings credit and honour, which support one's dignity; it furnishes help and subsistence to all broken men who are devoid of aught else.

W. (bliss) he enjoys who knows not suffering, sorrow nor anxiety, and has prosperity and happiness and a good enough house.

H. (hail) is the whitest of grain; it is whirled from the vault of heaven and is tossed about by gusts of wind and then it melts into water.

N. (trouble) is oppressive to the heart; yet often it proves a source of help and salvation to the children of men, to everyone who heeds it betimes.

I. (ice) is very cold and immeasurably slippery; it glistens as clear as glass and most like to gems; it is a floor wrought by the frost, fair to look upon.

characters, *calc* and *gar*, being invented to express the gutteral sounds. These later characters do not occur on the Thames scramasax or in any of the few inscriptions from the South of England, so it may be inferred that they were peculiar to Northumbria.

calc does not actually occur in Hickes, but is taken from Domit. A. IX. and Galba A. II.

19. *Gyfu* (Salzburg AS. *geofu*, Goth. *geuua*), *gumena*, abstract, "generosity."

22. Hickes, *Wen ne bruceð, ðe can weana lyt. Wenne*, dat. sg. of *wen*, not *wēn* (cf. Dom. A. IX.), a Kentish form of the *wyn* of the Salzburg Codex, Galba A. II. etc. (Sievers, *Anglia*, XIII. 4). As the name of the Runic W, *wyn* suits admirably in the passages of Cynewulf, e.g. Crist, v. 805, Elene, v. 1263, and is found elsewhere in AS. MSS., e.g. Elene, v. 1089, *on wuldres W*; Riddle XCI. 7, *modW*; Ps. Cos. XCIX. 1, *Wsumiaþ=jubilate*. From the Runic alphabet *wyn*, like *þorn*, was adopted into AS. script.

25. *Hægl* (Salz. AS. *haegil*, Goth. *haal*). Cf. *Hagall* in the Norwegian and Icelandic poems. The first two Runic characters in Hickes are taken from Domit. A. IX., the third alone belongs to the poem; cf. Hempl. *Mod. Phil.* I. 13.

26. *wealcaþ hit windes scura*; if *scur* can be fem. as Goth. *skura* (windis), ON. *skúr, scura*, N. pl., may be retained; otherwise it must be emended to *scuras*.

27. *Nyd* (Salzb. AS. *naed*, Goth. *noicz*?). Cf. Scandinavian poems and Elene, v. 1260: *N gefera   nearusorge dreah   enge rune*.

32 Ger byþ gumena hiht,   ðonne God læteþ,
　　halig heofones cyning,   hrusan syllan
　　beorhte bleda   beornum ond ðearfum.

35 Eoh byþ utan   unsmeþe treow,
　　heard hrusan fæst,   hyrde fyres,
　　wyrtrumun underwreþyd,   wyn on eþle.

38 Peorð byþ symble   plega and hlehter
　　wlancum [on middum],   ðar wigan sittaþ
　　on beorsele   bliþe ætsomne.

41 Eolh-secg eard hæfþ   oftust on fenne
　　wexeð on wature,   wundaþ grimme,
　　blode breneð   beorna gehwylcne
　　ðe him ænigne   onfeng gedeþ.

45 Sigel semannum   symble biþ on hihte,
　　ðonne hi hine feriaþ   ofer fisces beþ,
　　oþ hi brimhengest   bringeþ to lande.

32. H. *ðon.*   37. H. *wynan on eþle.*   39. *on middum* supplied
by Grein.   41. H. *eolhx seccard.*

32. *Ger* (Salz. OE. *gaer*, Goth. *gaar*)=summer.
Gear originally meant the warm part of the year (cf. Russian ярь,
"spring-corn"), parallel to *winter*; this meaning is occasionally found in
AS., e.g. Beowulf, v. 1134.   Then both *gear* and *winter* were used for
the whole year, though at a later time *winter* was restricted to its original
significance.
　　In Scandinavian *ár* came to denote the "products of the summer," hence
"plenty, abundance," e.g. *til árs ok friðar*, "for peace and plenty."
　　In the older alphabet the letter stood for J; but the initial *j*, falling
together with palatal *g* in AS., is almost invariably represented by the *gyfu*
letter in inscriptions. Cf., however, v. 87, *iar*.
35. *Eoh*: except in Runic alphabets this word is written *iw*, *se hearda
iw* of Riddle LVI. 9; but cf. OHG. *iha* beside *iwa*. The original form may
have been **ihwiz*. Hickes gives the value as *eo*, doubtless taken from
Domit. A. IX.   The value of the letter in the original alphabet is quite
unknown; but the Salzburg Codex has *ih* with the values *i* and *h*, and this
agrees with the only intelligible inscriptions in England in which the letter
occurs, viz. Dover: *Gislheard* (value *i*); Ruthwell: *Almehttig* (value *h*);
Thornhill II: *Eateinne* for *Eadþegne* (value *i*).
　　Eoh survived as *yogh*, *yok*, etc., the name of the ʒ letter in Middle
English. Cf. A. C. Paues, *M. L. R.* VI. 441 ff.
38. *Peorð* (Salzb. AS. *peord*, Goth. *pertra*). P was a rare sound in
the parent language. It is absent from the earliest Northern Inscriptions,
and in the alphabet from the Vadstena bracteate is represented by B. The
brooch from Charnay, Burgundy, has in this place a letter much resembling
the modern W, and in England it is found only in MS. lists of runic
characters and on coins (e.g. *Pada*, *Epa*), never in inscriptions.
　　Peorð is never found save as the name of the letter P, and no stress can
be laid on any of the suggested meanings. Leo, *As. Glossar.* Halle, 1877,

J.   (summer) is a joy to men, when God, the holy King of
     Heaven, suffers the earth to bring forth shining fruits
     for rich and poor alike.

I.   (the yew) is a tree with rough bark, hard and fast in
     the earth, supported by its roots, a guardian of flame
     and a joy upon an estate.

P.   (the chessman?) is a source of recreation and amuse-
     ment to the great, where warriors sit blithely together
     in the banqueting-hall.

Z.   (the ?-sedge) is mostly to be found in a marsh; it
     grows in the water and makes a ghastly wound,
     covering with blood every warrior who touches it.

S.   (the sun) is ever a joy to seafarers (or, in the hopes
     of seafarers) when they journey away over the fishes'
     bath, until the courser of the deep bears them to land.

compares Slav. *pizda* = vulva, W. Grimm the Icelandic *peð*, "a pawn in
chess." This latter suggestion is not regarded with much favour by
H. J. R. Murray in his *History of Chess*, p. 420 (Oxford, 1913).

41. Hickes, *Eolhx seccard hæfþ oftust on fenne.*

Grimm emends to *eolugsecg eard*, Grein to *eolx secg eard* and Rieger to
eolh secg eard, "the elk-sedge (sumpfgras als lager oder nährung des elches)
always grows in a marsh."

This letter, originally *z* (which disappeared finally, and became *r* elsewhere in AS.), is a fossil found only in Runic alphabets. An earlier form of
the name is seen in Epinal-Erfurt, 781, *papiluus*: *ilugsegg*, *ilugseg* (cf. the
ilcs of the Salzburg Codex), which cannot be connected with the word for
elk, and Wright-Wülker, *Voc.* 286. 36, *eolxsecg*: *papiluus*, where *papiluus*
probably = *papyrus.*

Cf. Epinal-Erfurt, 795, *paperum, papirum*: *eorisc.*

Corpus, 1503, *papirum*: *eorisc* (bulrush).

The subject of this stanza is therefore some rush, species unknown.

In this connection it is interesting to note that both *secg* and the Lat.
gladiolus, which it glosses in E.E. 463, and Corpus, 977, are derived from
words for sword; cf. Skeat, *Etymological Dictionary*, p. 546 (Oxford, 1910).

43. Hickes, *blode breneð.*

The natural way would be to take it as "browns (stains) with blood"
from *brun*; cf. Dante, *Inferno* xiii. 34, *Da che fatto fu poi di sangue
bruno*; but no such verb occurs in AS. or ON. *Breneð* (from *beornan*),
"burns with blood," makes no sense. A better interpretation is suggested
by a passage in Wulfstan, 183. 17 *Drihtnes rod bið blode beurnen*, "the
cross of the Lord is covered with blood." Possibly we should emend to
beerneð (though this verb does not actually occur) rather than to *beyrneð*.

45. *Sigel* (Salzb. AS. *sygil*, Goth. *sugil*) evidently "sun." Cf. Norwegian
and Icelandic *sól*. Moreover in the Exeter Book it is found at the beginning
and the end of Riddle vii., to which the answer is "the sun." Cf. Tupper,
Riddles of the Exeter Book, p. 81, and Wyatt, *Old English Riddles*
(frontispiece 2, 3).

46. *hine*, for *heonan*, hence, away; cf. Bede's Death Song, *v.* 1 *Ær his
hiniongae*. For the intrans. use of *ferian*, cf. Maldon, v. 179, etc.

48 Tir biþ tacna sum,   healdeð trywa wel
   wiþ æþelingas;   a biþ on færylde
   ofer nihta genipu,   næfre swiceþ.

51 Beorc byþ bleda leas,   bereþ efne swa ðeah
   tanas butan tudder,   biþ on telgum wlitig,
   *h*eah on helme   hrysted fægere,
   geloden leafum,   lyfte getenge.

55 Eh byþ for eorlum   æþelinga wyn,
   hors hofum wlanc,   ðær him hæleþ ymb[e]
   welege on wicgum   wrixlaþ. spræce
   and biþ unstyllum   æfre frofur.

59 Man byþ on myrgþe   his magan leof:
   sceal þeah anra gehwylc   oðrum swican,
   forðam drihten wyle   dome sine
   þæt earme flæsc   eorþan betæcan.

63 Lagu byþ leodum   langsum geþuht,
   gif hi sculun neþan   on nacan tealtum
   and hi sæyþa   swyþe bregaþ
   and se brimhengest   bridles ne gym[eð].

53. H. *þeah.*	**56.** H. *ymb.*	**59.** H. *deg* inserted above *man.*
60. H. *odrum.*	**64.** H. *neþun.*	**66.** H. *gym.*

48. *Tir* (Salzb. AS. *Ti.* Goth. *Tyz*).
There can be no doubt that the original name of this letter was *Ti* (*Tiw*)
from **Tiwaz*, cf. ON. *Týr*, pl. *tivar* This word appears in glosses, e.g.
Epinal-Erfurt, 663, Corpus, 1293, *Mars, Martis*: *Tiig*, and most of the
Teutonic peoples use it as a translation of *Martis*, in the third day of the
week. It is natural therefore to suppose that *Tir* is a misreading for *Tiw*.
If *tacna sum*=star, one would expect it to be the planet Mars ♂; but the
description of the poem is appropriate rather to "a circumpolar constella-
tion" (Botkine). Possibly the poet had in his mind a word different from
the original name of the letter.
Cf. ON. *týri* (?): *lumen* (Egilsson, *Lexicon Poet.* s.v.). E.g. Leiðarvisan,
v. 14, *harri heims týriss*; "King of the light of the world."
51. *Beorc* (Salz. AS. *berc*, Goth. *bercna*; cf. ON. *bjarkan*). The
customary meaning "birch" is here unsuitable; but according to the
glossaries it can mean "poplar" too,
                e.g. Epinal-Erfurt, 792, *populus* : *birciae*.
                    Corpus, 1609, *populus* : *birce*.
            Wright, *Voc.* I. 33. 2, 80.13, *byrc* : *populus*.
        Anecdota Oxon., 56, 364, 365, *byric* : *populus, betula*.
   byþ bleda leas. Doubless popular science. Cf. Evelyn, *Silva* (London,
1908), I. 128 : "I begin the second class with the poplar, of which there are
several kinds; white, black, etc., which in Candy 'tis reported bears seeds."
It is a fact, however, that poplars are almost always grown from slips or
suckers. For instance, Mr H. J. Elwes declares that he has never found in
England a poplar grown from seed either naturally or by nurserymen, that

T. (?) is a (guiding) star; well does it keep faith
with princes; it is ever on its course over the mists
of night and never fails.

B. (the poplar) bears no fruit; yet without seed it brings
forth suckers, for it is generated from its leaves.
Splendid are its branches and gloriously adorned its
lofty crown which reaches to the skies.

E. (the horse) is a joy to princes in the presence of
warriors, a steed in the pride of its hoofs, when
rich men on horseback bandy words about it; and
it is ever a source of comfort to the restless.

M. the joyous (man) is dear to his kinsmen; yet every
man is doomed to fail his fellow, since the Lord
by his decree will commit the vile carrion to the
earth.

L. (the ocean) seems interminable to men, if they venture
on the rolling bark and the waves of the sea terrify
them and the courser of the deep heed not its
bridle.

moreover no good description or illustration of the germination of poplars seems
to have been published in England before that of Miss F. Woolward in 1907;
cf. Elwes and Henry, *The Trees of Great Britain and Ireland*, vol. VII.
pp. 1770 ff. (Edinburgh, 1913).

The grey poplar (*populus canescens*), indigenous to England and Western
Europe, is a large tree attaining 100 ft or more in height (*lyfte getenge*) and
15 ft in girth.

55. *Eh*, as the Salzburg Codex. Cf. Gothic *aihwatundi*, Lat. *equus*,
Greek ἵππος; value E in the original alphabet and in AS.

In Scandinavian, however, the word became *jór* and the letter disappeared, E being represented by I. Later still a dotted I was introduced
to differentiate between E and I.

56. Hickes *ymb*, emended to *ymbe*, metri gratia (Sievers, *P.B.B.*, x. 519).

59. *Man* (Salzburg AS. *mon*, Goth. *manna*). Cf. p. 32, l. 1 (Icelandic
poem), *Maðr er manns gaman ok moldar auki.*

Above the correct value *m* Hickes engraves *d. deg.*, doubtless taken from
Domit. A. IX. Cf. v. 74, *Dæg*.

The Runic character for M is used fairly often in the Lindisfarne Gospels
and the Rituale of Durham, once too in the preface to the Rushworth
Gospels, *FarM* for *Farman* (e.g. *Surtees Society*, Stevenson, *Rituale
Ecclesiae Dunelmensis*, 1840; Stevenson and Waring, *The Lindisfarne and
Rushworth Gospels*, 4 vols., 1854–1865). It is found moreover in the Exeter
Book, e.g. Ruin, v. 24, *Mdreama* for *mandreama*.

63. *Lagu*, sea, cf. OS. *lagu-* in compounds, ON. *lǫgr.* (Salzburg Codex
AS. *lagu*, Goth. *laaz*.)

The same meaning is found in the Runic passages of Cynewulf, Crist,
v. 807, Elene, v. 1268, Fates of the Apostles, II. v. 7.

66. *ne gym[eð]*. Hickes, *negym*, the last two letters being doubtless
illegible in the MS.

67 Ing wæs ærest   mid East-Denum
      gesewen secgun,   oþ he siððan est
      ofer wæg gewat;   wæn æfter ran;
      ðus Heardingas   ðone hæle nemdun.

71 Eþel byþ oferleof   æghwylcum men,
      gif he mot ðær rihtes   and gerysena on
      brucan on bolde   bleadum oftast.

74 Dæg byþ drihtnes sond,   deore mannum,
      mære metodes leoht,   myrgþ and tohiht
      eadgum and earmum,   eallum‚brice.

77 Ac byþ on eorþan   elda bearnum
      flæsces fodor,   fereþ gelome
      ofer ganotes bæþ;   garsecg fandaþ
      hwæþer ac hæbbe   æþele treowe.

73. H. *blode.*   74. H. *mann* inserted above *dæg.*

67. *Ing* (Salzb. AS. *Ing*, Goth. *Enguz*), the letter for *ng* in the original
alphabet; occasionally it is used for *ing*, e.g. *Birᵹngu* on the stone from
Opedal, Norway; Ing is doubtless the eponym of the Ingwine, a name
applied to the Danes in Beowulf, vv. 1044, 1319, where Hrothgar is styled
eodor Ingwina, frean Ingwina.
　　The earliest reference to Ing is to be found in the Ingaevones of Tacitus,
c. II., and Pliny, whom Professor Chadwick (*Origin of the English Nation,*
pp. 207 ff.) has shown there is some reason for identifying with the con-
federation of Baltic tribes who worshipped Nerthus, *id est Terra Mater,*
on an island in the ocean, perhaps the Danish isle of Sjælland. But in
later times the name is almost exclusively confined to Sweden; e.g.
Arngrim Jónsson's epitome of the Skiöldunga saga (Olrik, *Aarb.f.n.O.,*
1894, p. 105): *tradunt Odinum...Daniam...Scioldo, Sveciam Ingoni filiis
assignasse. Atque inde a Scioldo, quos hodie Danos, olim Skiolldunga fuisse
appellatos; ut et Svecos ab Ingoni Inglinga.* In Icelandic literature, e.g. the
Ynglinga saga, the name Ynglingar is applied to the Swedish royal family,
and the god Frey, their favourite divinity and reputed ancestor, is himself
styled Yngvi-Freyr and Ingunar freyr (the lord of the prosperity of the
Ingwine or the husband of Ingun). It is significant, moreover, that the
name of his father Njǫrðr is phonetically equivalent to Nerthus, and his own
cult as a god of peace and prosperity is evidently descended from that of the
selfsame goddess (cf. Chadwick, *O. E. N.* p. 230 ff.).
　　69. *wæn æfter ran,* doubtless to be connected with the following passages,
Tacitus, *Germania,* c. XL: *They have a common worship of Nerthus, that is
Mother Earth, and believe that she intervenes in human affairs and visits the
nations in her car,* etc., and the story of Gunnarr Helmingr in the Flateyjarbók Saga of Olaf Tryggvason, which relates that there was in Sweden an
image of the god Freyr, which in winter time was carried about the country
in a car, *gera mǫnnum árbót,* to bring about an abundant season for men;
cf. Vigfússon and Unger, *Flateyjarbók,* I. 338, translated in Sephton's *Saga
of K. Olaf Tryggvason,* p. 258 ff.
　　70. *Heardingas,* not elsewhere in AS., perhaps a generic term for
"warriors" as in Elene, vv. 25, 130. It corresponds however to the ON.
Haddingjar and the *Asdingi,* a section of the Vandals (from *haddr,* "a

NG. (Ing) was first seen by men among the East-Danes, till, followed by his car, he departed eastwards over the waves. So the Heardingas named the hero.

Œ. (an estate) is very dear to every man, if he can enjoy there in his house whatever is right and proper in constant prosperity.

D. (day), the glorious light of the Creator, is sent by the Lord; it is beloved of men, a source of hope and happiness to rich and poor, and of service to all.

A. (the oak) fattens the flesh (of swine) for the children of men. Often it traverses the gannet's bath, and the ocean proves whether the oak keeps faith in honourable fashion.

coiffure"; cf. Tacitus' account of the Suevi, *Germ.* c. xxxviii.). The term *skati Haddingja*, "prince of the H.," is used in Kalfsvisa (Skaldskaparmál, c. lviii.), and is applied to Helgi, the reincarnation of Helgi Hundingsbani, in the prose which follows Helgakviþa Hundingsbana ii.

In two of the Fornaldar Sögur, Hrómundarsaga Greipssonar, c. vi., and Örvar-Oddssaga, c. xiv., Haddingi is a personal name; and in Saxo, Bk i. (Holder, p. 19 ff.), mention is made of a Hadingus, King of the Danes, whose visit to the nether world is probably alluded to in the phrase from Guþrúnarkviþa hin forna, c. xxiii., *lands Haddingja áx óskorit.* It is worthy of note, moreover, that the verses (Gylf, c. xxiii.) in which Njǫrðr and Skaði bewail their incompatibility of temperament are by Saxo (Holder, p. 33) attributed to Hadingus and his wife. On the whole it seems most satisfactory to regard *Heardingas* as the name of a people or a dynasty, conceivably the North Suevi; for Saxo, at any rate, derives fictitious personages from national or dynastic names, cf. *Hothbroddus*, Bk ii. (Holder, p. 52), and the *Heaðobeardan* of Beowulf, vv. 2032 ff.

71. *Eþel* (Salzburg AS. *oedil*, Goth. *utal*), originally perhaps *ōþila, the name of the O letter in the original alphabet. Cf. Golden Horn of Gallehus (Jutland), HORNA TAWIÐO; English coin from British Museum, SKANOMODU. In AS. it became *œþel* (WS. *eþel*) and the letter changed its value to *œ*, e.g. Ruthwell Cross, LIMWŒRIGNÆ. This letter is occasionally found in AS. mss. as a grammalogue for *eþel*, e.g. Waldhere, v. 31, Beowulf, v. 520, 913, 1702.

74. *Dæg* (Salz. AS. *daeg*, Goth. *daaz*). Hickes, following the ignorant scribe of Dom. A. ix., inserts *m, mann*, above the correct value *d*.

The Runic letter D is regularly found as a grammalogue for *dæg* in the Rituale of Durham, occasionally too in the Lindisfarne Gospels.

77. *Ac* (< *aik-), doubtless a ligature of A and I, the first of the characters introduced to express the sound-changes which differentiated AS. from the language of the earliest Northern inscriptions.

elda bearnum flœsces fodor, acorns, as the food of swine, since pork was the flesh most commonly eaten in AS. times. For an illustration of swine feeding in an oak-forest, cf. AS. calendar for September, Cott. Tib. B. v., Jul. A. vi.

For the second part of the stanza, cf. Egill Skallagrimsson's *Höfuðlausn*, str. i., "*Drók eik á flot við ísabrot*" (Egilssaga, c. ix.).

81 Æsc biþ oferheah, eldum dyre
   stiþ on staþule, stede rihte hylt,
   ðeah him feohtan on firas monige.

84 Yr byþ æþelinga *and* eorla gehwæs
   wyn and wyrþmynd, byþ on wicge fæger,
   fæstlic on færelde, fyrdgeatewa sum.

87 Iar byþ eafix and ðeah a bruceþ
   fodres on foldan, hafaþ fægerne eard
   wætre beworpen, ðær he wynnum leofaþ.

90 Ear byþ egle eorla gehwylcun,
   ðonn[e] fæstlice flæsc onginneþ,
   hraw colian, hrusan ceosan
   blac to gebeddan ; bleda gedreosaþ,
   wynna gewitaþ, wera geswicaþ.

---

86. H. *fyrdgeacewa*.   87. H. *eafixa*.   88. H. *onfaldan*.
91. *ðonn*. At the end of Hickes' transcript there stand four runes to
which no verses are attached, *cw, cweorð; c* [*calc*]; *st, stan; g, gar*. Two
of these Runic letters, *calc* and *gar*, are found on the Ruthwell Cross in the
value of guttural *c* and *g*.

81. *Æsc*, identical in form with A (**ansuz*), the fourth letter of the
older alphabet, since in the majority of cases original *a* became *æ* in AS.
84. *Yr* (Salzb. *yr*). The Runic passages in Cynewulf give no assistance
and the meaning is much disputed. The new edition of Grein's *Sprachschatz* translates "horn," I know not upon what evidence unless it be the
parallel phraseology of Riddle xv. Others have identified it with the ON.
ýr, "bow," cf. p. 32; but this corresponds to AS. *eoh*, p. 16. Is it possible
to connect AS. *yr* with the word *æxe-yre* in the Chronicle 1012 E, translated
by Plummer "axe-head," "axe-iron"? We might compare *Ýr er...brotgjarnt
jarn* in the Icelandic poem, p. 32.
87. Hickes, *Iar* (*io*) *bið ea fixa, and ðeah abruceþ*. Following Dom. A.
ix. and Galba A. ii., W. Grimm emends to *Ior*.
As it stands *eafixa* is a Gen. pl. with nothing on which to depend, and
the addition of *sum* (Grein) would render the verse unmetrical. The final *a*
of *eafixa* should therefore be deleted (Rieger).
abruceþ Grimm. *a bruceþ*, "always enjoys."
This letter is not in the Salzburg Codex.
No such word as *iar, ior* exists; but the description here given is plainly
that of some amphibious creature, usually taken as the eel (Grimm), though
it might equally well be a lizard or newt (*aðexe, efete*).
It is worth remarking that the letter is used in a number of Scandinavian
inscriptions from the seventh century onwards, e.g. Bjorketorp, Stentofte,
Gommor (Blekinge) and Vatn (Norway), seventh cent. ; Kallerup, Snoldelev,
Flemlöse (Denmark) and Örja (Skaane), early ninth cent., as a form of
the letter *ár* (*a*). The original value of this was *j*; moreover it occurs in
two English inscriptions : Dover, GISLHEARD ; Thornhill III, GILSUITH,
with the value of palatal *g*, since palatal *g* and original *j* had fallen together
at an early date in AS.

Æ. (the ash) is exceedingly high and precious to men. With its sturdy trunk it offers a stubborn resistance, though attacked by many a man.

Y. (?) is a source of joy and honour to every prince and knight; it looks well on a horse and is a reliable equipment for a journey.

IO. (?) is a river fish and yet it always feeds on land; it has a fair abode encompassed by water, where it lives in happiness.

EA. (the grave ?) is horrible to every knight, when the corpse quickly begins to cool and is laid in the bosom of the dark earth. Prosperity declines, happiness passes away and covenants are broken.

There appears to be no reason for doubting that this is a survival of the twelfth letter (*j*) of the older alphabet. Is it possible then that *iar* (*ior*) is a corrupt form of the name *gear*? Cf. v. 32 (Chadwick). In that case we must of course assume that the poet had some other name in his mind, e.g. eel, newt.

90. *Ear* (Salzb. *eor*, value *eo*); this word is only found in Runic alphabets. Grein compares ON. *aurr*, a poetical word which seems to mean loam or clay (cf. Vǫluspá xix. 2, Alvíssmál xix. 4, Rígsþula x. 3, Grottasǫngr xvi. 3), hence "ground" in the sense of "grave."

The letter is fairly common in inscriptions, e.g. Dover, GISLHE*A*RD, Thames scramasax, B*EA*GNOTH, and often in Northumbria. In Northumbrian inscriptions it is used for *eo* as well as for *ea*, doubtless owing to the fact that these diphthongs were confused in Northumbria.

THE NORWEGIAN RUNIC POEM

1 Fé vældr frænda róge;
     fǿðesk ulfr í skóge.

2 Úr er af illu jarne;
     opt lǿypr ræinn á hjarne.

3 Þurs vældr kvinna kvillu;
     kátr værðr fár af illu.

4 Óss er flæstra færða
     fǫr; en skalpr er sværða.

5 Ræið kveða rossom væsta;
     Reginn sló sværðet bæzta.

6 Kaun er barna bǫlvan;
     bǫl gǫrver nán fǫlvan.

7 Hagall er kaldastr korna;
     Kristr skóp hæimenn forna.

1. *Fé.* The Runic characters for F and M are used in Icelandic MSS. for *fé* and *maðr*; cf. Jónsson, *Oldnorske Litteraturs Historie* II. 254. *frænda róge*, a kenning for gold; cf. *rógi Niflunga*, Bjarkamál, v. 19, etc.

fǿðesk ulfr í skóge. Cf. Cott. Gnomic Verses, v. 11: *wulf sceal on bearowe.*

2. *Úr.* Cf. Jón Olafsson, *Runologia* (Add. 8 fol. p. 141): *Sunnlendingar kalla smidiu uur, þat Nordlingar smidiu giall,* "people in the S. of Iceland call *úr* what the Northerners call slag, the refuse from a smith's furnace." This is supported by a passage in the þáttr af Gull-Ásu-þorði, c. VI. (ed. Jónsson, XL. *Islendinga þættir*, p. 83, Reykjavík, 1904), *Úrt járn, kvað kerlingr, ok atti kneif deigan.* [*Småstykker*, p. 100, cf. pp. 106, 112.]

3. *þurs.* As against the AS. *þorn* (found twice in the grammatical treatises attached to the Prose Edda, *Edda Snorra Sturlusonar* II. 38, 365), all Scandinavian Runic alphabets have *þurs*, the first element in such personal names as the Gothic Thorismund and the Gepide Thurisind; the earliest form of this word is the *thuris* of Hrabanus Maurus' *Abecedarium Nordmannicum*, see p. 34.

kvinna kvillu, kvilla=kvilli, sickness, ailment, freq. in mod. usage (Cleasby-Vigfússon). In their *Corpus Poeticum Boreale* II. 370, Vigfússon and Powell translate the phrase "hysterics," perhaps on the strength of Skírnismál XXXVII.:

    þurs rístk þér   ok þria stafi:
    ergi ok ǿþi ok óþola;
    svá af rístk   sem þat á reistk,
    ef gǫrvask þarfar þess.

4. *Óss*, orig.<*Ansuz, like the AS. *os*, perhaps perverted from its original significance by ecclesiastical influence in Norway as in England.

The text requires some emendation; Worm's *Oys er flestra ferda, En skalpur er sverda* has obviously lost a syllable; and Magnússon's *Óss er læid flestra færda, En skalper er sværda*, though translateable, is unmetrical.

THE NORWEGIAN RUNIC POEM

1 Wealth is a source of discord among kinsmen;
the wolf lives in the forest.

2 Dross comes from bad iron;
the reindeer often races over the frozen snow.

3 *Giant* causes anguish to women;
misfortune makes few men cheerful.

4 Estuary is the way of most journeys;
but a scabbard is of swords.

5 Riding is said to be the worst thing for horses;
Reginn forged the finest sword.

6 Ulcer is fatal to children;
death makes a corpse pale.

7 Hail is the coldest of grain;
Christ created the world of old.

Kålund, therefore, substitutes for *læið* the synonym *fǫr* (so AM. 739 4to, a MS. collection of Edda excerpts, in which Worm's version of the poem is preserved), and places it at the beginning of the second line. Bugge and Ólsen, however, regarding *fǫr*, a short syllable, as metrically doubtful, suggest *færill*, yet a third synonym. [*Småstykker*, p. 101.]

5. *Ræið*. Cf. AS. poem, v. 13 ff.

Reginn, son of Hreiðmarr, who received the "Otter-price" from the Aesir, and brother of the serpent Fáfnir, who brooded over the gold on Gnita-heath. He fostered Sigurd, forged for him the sword Gramr and persuaded him to slay the dragon, but was slain by Sigurd, who suspected treachery. Cf. Reginsmál, Fáfnismál, Skaldsk. cc. xxxix.–xl. and Vǫlsunga saga cc. xiii.–xix., *sværðet bæzta*; cf. Skaldsk. c. xl.: *þa gǫrði Reginn sverð þat er Gramr heitir, er svá var hvast at Sigurðr brá niðr í rennanda vatn, ok tók í sundr ullarlagð, er rak fyrir strauminum at sverðseggini. því næst klauf Sigurðr steðja Regins ofan í stokkinn með sverðinu.*

6. AM, JE,   *Kaun er beggja barna*
                bol gorvir naan folfvan,
which Bugge would retain, "An ulcer is fatal to children of both sexes; it makes a corpse pale." Olsen, comparing *kaun er barna böl* of the Icelandic poem, and Landnámabók (*Isl.* i. 1526) *böl gjörir mik fölvan*, would emend to

    Kaun er barna bǫlvan;   "An ulcer is fatal to children;
        bǫl gǫrver man fǫlvan.   death makes a man pale."

[*Småstykker*, p. 101.] But while accepting the emendation of the first line, I do not think it necessary to alter the MS. reading of the second.

7. *kaldastr korna*. Cf. AS. poem, v. 25, *Hægl byþ hwitust corna*, and Seafarer, v. 32, *hægl feol on eorðan, corna caldast.*

Kristr. Christ was sometimes regarded as the Creator. Cf. Skaldsk. c. li.: *Hvernig skal Krist kalla? Svá at kalla hann skapara himins ok jarðar*, etc.

8 Nauðr gerer næppa koste ;
   nǫktan kælr í froste.

9 Ís kǫllum brú bræiða;
   blindan þarf at læiða.

10 Ár er gumna góðe ;
   get ek at ǫrr var Fróðe.

11 Sól er landa ljóme ;
   lúti ek helgum dóme.

12 Týr er æinendr ása ;
   opt værðr smiðr blása.

13 Bjarkan er laufgrønstr líma ;
   Loki bar flærða tíma.

14 Maðr er moldar auki ;
   mikil er græip á hauki.

15 Lǫgr er, fællr ór fjalle
   foss; en gull ero nosser.

16 Ýr er vetrgrønstr viða ;
   vænt er, er brennr, at sviða.

8. *Nauðr.* For use of the letter in magic, cf. Sigrdrífumál VII. :
   Ölrunar skalt kunna ef þu vill annars kvǽn
      vélit þik i trygþ, ef trúir;
   á horni skalt rista ok á handa baki
      ok merkja á nagli Nauþ.
9. *Ís kǫllum brú bræiða.* Cf. Exeter Gnomic Verses, v. 72 ff. :
   Forst sceal freosan...is brycgian,
      wæterhelm wegan,
and Andreas, v. 1260 ff.
10. *Ár*, descended, like the AS. *gear*, from the old *j* letter (*jāra). It
means (1) year, (2) summer, cf. *gear* in Beowulf, v. 1136, (3) what summer
brings, harvest, (4) prosperity, especially in the phrase *til árs ok friðar*, for
peace and prosperity.
   Fróðe, Friðleifsson (Frotho III of Saxo, Bk v.), the peace-king of Danish
legend who is made a contemporary of Augustus. So great was the security
in his days that a gold ring lay out for many years on Jællinge Heath.
Fróði owned the quern Grotti, which ground for him gold or whatsoever
else he wished; hence gold is called by the skaldic poets *Fróða mjöl*,
"Froði's meal." Cf. Skaldsk. c. XLII. ; Skjöldunga saga c. III. [Chadwick,
Origin of the English Nation, p. 257 ff.]
12. *Týr*, originally "the god," cf. Lat. *divus* ; the pl. *Tivar* is used as
a generic name for the gods in the Older Edda. In the Prose Edda (Gylf
c. XXV.) he is the god of war, but most of his functions have been usurped
by Othin and he is a character of small importance in Scandinavian religion
as it has come down to us.

8 Constraint gives scant choice;
  a naked man is chilled by the frost.

9 Ice we call the broad bridge;
  the blind man must be led.

10 Plenty is a boon to men;
  I say that Frothi was generous.

11 Sun is the light of the world;
  I bow to the divine decree.

12 Tyr is a one-handed god;
  often has the smith to blow.

13 Birch has the greenest leaves of any shrub;
  Loki was fortunate in his deceit.

14 Man is an augmentation of the dust;
  great is the claw of the hawk.

15 A waterfall is a River which falls from a mountain-side;
  but ornaments are of gold.

16 Yew is the greenest of trees in winter;
  it is wont to crackle when it burns.

æinendr, because he offered his right hand as a pledge to the *Fenrisulfr*, who promptly bit it off when he found himself securely bound with the fetter Gleipnir (Gylf. c. xxxiv.). Cf. Sigrdrífumál vi.:

> *Sigrúnar skalt kunna,*   *ef vill sigr hafa,*
>   *ok rísti á hjalti hjǫrs,*
> *sumar á véttrimum,*   *sumar á valbǫstum*
>   *ok nefna tysvar Tý.*

13. *Bjarkan* (= *björk*, birch), found only as the name of the letter B in the Runic alphabet.

Loki bar flærða tíma is not perhaps very satisfactory; it will translate, however, if *bar tíma* be taken in the sense of *bera gæfu til*, to be fortunate in; cf. Ólsen and Bugge, *Småstykker*, pp. 102, 111. So it seems unnecessary to accept the *C.P.B.* emendation, *Loki brá flærða síma*.

The reference is doubtless to Loki's responsibility for Balder's death. Gylf. c. xlix.

14. *Maðr er moldar auki.* Cf. Hervarar saga c. v. 3:

> *Mjök eruð orðnir*   *Arngrims synir*
>   *megir at meinsamir*   *moldar auki,*

probably from Psalm cii. 14.

15. Construe; *foss er lǫgr fællr ór fjalle.*
nosser. Icelandic *hnossir.*

16. It is worth noting that *ýr* is phonetically equivalent to the AS. *eoh* (*ih*), though the character which bears that name is apparently descended from the fifteenth letter of the old alphabet (*eolh-secg*), which in Scandinavian inscriptions from the sixth century onwards (e.g. Kragehul, Stentofte, etc.) is inverted.

THE ICELANDIC RUNIC POEM

1 Fé er frænda róg
   ok flæðar viti
   ok grafseiðs gata
     aurum   fylkir.

2 Úr er skýja grátr
   ok skára þverrir
   ok hirðis hatr.
     umbre   vísi.

3 Þurs er kvenna kvöl
   ok kletta búi
   ok varðrúnar verr.
     Saturnus   þengill.

4 Óss er aldingautr
   ok ásgarðs jǫfurr,
   ok valhallar vísi.
     Jupiter   oddviti.

5 Reið er sitjandi sæla
   ok snúðig ferð
   ok jórs erfiði.
     iter   ræsir.

6 Kaun er barna böl
   ok bardaga [för]
   ok holdfúa hús
     flagella   konungr.

---

1. *flæðar viti*, AM. 687; *fyrða gaman*, 461, 749, JO *b*; *Fofnis bani*, JO *a*. Cf. *þorðar saga Hræða* c. vi., *viti leifnis lautar; ignis maris* (Egilsson).

grafseiðs gata, lit. "path of the grave-fish" (*seiðr: pisciculus*, Egilsson), a kenning for gold from the connection of dragons and other serpents with graves containing treasure. Cf. Bjarkamál, v. 19, *Grafvitnis dúnn*; Harmsól, v. 44, *dælar seiðs dunn*.

aurum, etc. (from 687), more or less accurate equivalents in Latin of the letter names.

fylkir, etc. (from 687), a series of synonyms for "king," each of which alliterates with the stanza to which it is attached; with the exception of *oddviti* they are to be found in the *þulor* (rhymed glossaries) printed in *C. P. B.* II. 422 ff.

2. *skýja grátr*. Cf. Ragnars saga Loðbrókar, c. xxi. (*FAS.* I. 224),
     nu skýtr á mik   skýja grátr.

THE ICELANDIC RUNIC POEM

1 Wealth = source of discord among kinsmen
   and fire of the sea
   and path of the serpent.

2 Shower = lamentation of the clouds
   and ruin of the hay-harvest
   and abomination of the shepherd.

3 Giant = torture of women
   and cliff-dweller
   and husband of a giantess.

4 God = aged Gautr
   and prince of Asgard
   and lord of Valhalla.

5 Riding = joy of the horseman
   and speedy journey
   and toil of the steed.

6 Ulcer = disease fatal to children
   and painful spot
   and abode of mortification.

skára þverrir. Wimmer reads *skara þverrir,* " der eisränder auflöser,"
from *skǫr,* "edge of the ice"; but *skára* (cf. Haldorsen, *Lexicon Islandico-
Latino-Danicum,* Havniae 1814, *skári: circulus qui uno ictu falcis metitur,*
"swathe") is metrically preferable. (*Småstykker,* p 111.)

umbre, obviously a mistake for *imber.* Cf. AM. 687, p. 3, *Ymber skúr,
skúr er úr, úr er rúnastafr* (Wimmer, p. 287).

3. *kletta búi.* Cf. Hymiskviþa II. *bergbúi,* cliff-dweller, a common
kenning for giant.

Varðrún, a giantess in the *Nafnaþulor, Snorra Edda,* ed. Jónsson, p. 269.
AM. 749 has *síðförull seggr.*

4. *aldingautr,* an epithet of Othin, the original meaning of which had
probably been forgotten at the time of the poem's composition. Cf. Veg-
tamskviþa II., *Upp reis Oþinn aldinn gautr* (according to Gering "redner,"
"sprecher"? "ancient sage"?). More probably *Gautr* is to be taken as
"god of the Gautar" (the Geatas of Beowulf), cf. Grimnismál LIV., *Gautr*;
Sonatorrek, v. 4: *Hergautr; Valgautr,* etc., an abbreviation of the *Gauta-
Týr* found in Hákonarmál, v. 1.

Othin is always depicted as an old man.

For *ásgarð* and *valhǫll* see the Prose Edda passim.

valhallar vísi. Cf. Bugge, *Småstykker,* p. 112.

5. *Reið.* Cf. Rad in the Anglo-Saxon poem, p. 14.

jórs, classical Icelandic *jós.*

6. 687, 461, 749, JO *a,* read *bardagi* alone, accepted by Wimmer.
JO *b,* however, has *bardaga för,* which Bugge, *Småstykker,* p. 111, takes in
the sense of "et sted, hvor Plage (Smerte) færdes (holder til)."

7 Hagall er kaldakorn
   ok krapadrífa
   ok snáka sótt
    grando   hildingr.

8 Nauð er þýjar þrá
   ok þungr kostr
   ok vássamlig verk.
    opera   niflungr.

9 Íss er árbörkr
   ok unnar þak
   ok feigra manna fár
    glacies   jöfurr.

10 Ár er gumna góði
   ok gott sumar
   ok algróinn akr
    annus   allvaldr.

11 Sól er skýja skjöldr
   ok skínandi röðull
   ok ísa aldrtregi
    rota   siklingr.

12 Týr er einhendr áss
   ok ulfs leifar
   ok hofa hilmir
    Mars   tiggi.

13 Bjarkan er laufgat lim
   ok lítit tré
   ok ungsamligr viðr
    abies   buðlungr.

---

7. *snáka sótt*, sickness of serpents, a kenning for winter. Cf. *naðra deyði* in Ívarr Ingimundarson, *C. P. B.* II. 264.

8. Cf. Grottasǫngr, especially strophe XVI. :

    Nu erum komnar   til konungs húsa
    miskunnlausar   ok at mani hafþar ;
    aurr etr iljar,   en ofan kulþi,
    drǫgum dolgs sjǫtul ;   daprt's at Fróþar.

þrá, aegritudo animi, maeror (Haldorsen).
þungr kostr, 749, JO. *þvera erfiði*, 461, illegible in 687.

9. *árbörkr*, illegible in 687.

7　Hail = cold grain
　　and shower of sleet
　　and sickness of serpents.

8　Constraint = grief of the bond-maid
　　and state of oppression
　　and toilsome work.

9　Ice = bark of rivers
　　and roof of the wave
　　and destruction of the doomed.

10　Plenty = boon to men
　　and good summer
　　and thriving crops.

11　Sun = shield of the clouds
　　and shining ray
　　and destroyer of ice.

12　Tyr = god with one hand
　　and leavings of the wolf
　　and prince of temples.

13　Birch = leafy twig
　　and little tree
　　and fresh young shrub.

unnar þak, 461, 749, JO *b*: doubtful in 687; *unnar þekja*, JO *a*.
Cf. Grettis saga, c. LII., *i marþaks miðjum firði* (in the midst of Isafjörðr,
Icefirth).
　feigra manna fár, 687; *feigs fár*, JO *a*; *feigs manns forað*, 461; *feigs
forað*, 749, JO *b*; cf. Fáfnismál IV., *alt er feigs forað*. With the use of this
phrase as a kenning for "ice," cf. Málsháttakvæði, v. 25, *sjaldan hittisk
feigs vǫk frǿrin* (Wimmer).
　10. *gott sumar*, 749, JO *a*; doubtful in 687; *glatt s.*, JO *b*.
　algróinn akr, 749, JO; *ok vel flest þat er vill*, 461; 687 has *dala*
(doubtful) *dreyri*, "moisture of the dales," i.e. *ár*, N. pl. of *á*, "river"
(Wimmer).
　11. *skýja skjöldr*. Cf. þórsdrápa, v. 13, *himintarga* (*C.P.B.* II. 19).
749 and JO have, in place of *ísa aldrtregi*, *hverfandi hvél*, "circling wheel,"
cf. *rota*.
　12. *hofa hilmir*. Cf. Haraldssaga Hárfagra, c. IX. 1 *hilmir vébrautar*:
praeses fani, rex (Egilsson).
　13. *ungsamligr*. Bugge reads *vegsamligr*, "glorious," in place of
ungsamligr, which is not found either in old or modern Icelandic.
(*Småstykker*), p. 112.

14   Maðr er manns gaman
         ok moldar auki
         ok skipa skreytir
             homo   mildingr.

15   Lögr er vellanda vatn
         ok víðr ketill
         ok glömmungr grund.
             lacus   lofðungr.

16   Ýr er bendr bogi
         ok brotgjarnt járn
         ok fífu fárbauti
             arcus   ynglingr.

14. *Maðr er manns gaman.* This phrase occurs also in Hávamál xlvii., whence it is doubtless borrowed.

skipa skreytir. Cf. *Fornmanna sǫgur* xi. 187. *skautreina skreytir : exornator navium* (Egilsson).

15. *vellanda vatn*, 687 ; all other texts have *vellandi vimr* (i.e. *vimur*), "hervorquellende flut." Cf. the Norwegian poem (Wimmer).

glömmungr, name of a fish in the *þulor, Snorra Edda*, p. 286.

16. *Ýr.* The character found here is regularly used for Y in the Icelandic inscriptions, none of which are much earlier than 1300. Cf. Kålund, *Aarb. f. n. O.* 1882, p. 98 ff.

brotgjarnt járn = ýr, a different word from *ýr*, bow. Cf. *úr* of the Norwegian poem, *kaldyr* of Merlinusspá and *kaldór = ferrum fragile* of Haldorsen (Wimmer).

14   Man = delight of man
       and augmentation of the earth
       and adorner of ships.

15   Water = eddying stream
       and broad geysir
       and land of the fish.

16   $\acute{Y}r$ = bent bow
       and brittle iron
       and giant of the arrow.

---

brotgjarnt = brittle.   Cf. Egill Skallagrimsson's *Arinbjarnar drápa*, v. 1 :

     hlóðk lofköst   þanns lengi stendr
     óbrotgjarnt   í bragar túni
     (exegi monumentum aere perennius).

For *brotgjarnt járn*, 749 has *bardaga gangr*, "journey of battle"; JO *b*, *bardaga gagn*, "implement of battle."

Fífu fárbauti, JO *b*; *fífa*, poetical word for "arrow".; cf. *þulor, Snorra Edda*, p. 281.

Fárbauti, a giant, father of the god Loki, Gylf. c. xxxiii., Skm. c. xvi., hence in poetry a generic term for giant.   749 has *fenju fleygir*, "speeder of the arrow."

APPENDIX

Abecedarium Nordmannicum.

From Codex Sangallensis 878, fol. 321, a 9th century MS. of Hrabanus Maurus containing the earliest example of the sixteen letter alphabet of the Viking Age. Cf. Mullenhoff and Scherer, *Denkmäler deutscher Poesie und Prosa*₍₃₎ p. 19 (Berlin, 1892); for facsimile, Wimmer, *Die Runenschrift*, p. 236:—

> Feu forman,
> Ûr after,
> Thuris thritten stabu,
> Os ist *hi*mo oboro,
> Rat endost ritan
> Cha*on* thanne cliuôt.
> Hagal, Nau*t* hab&
> Is, Ar endi Sol,
> *Tiu*, Brica endi Man midi
> Lago the leohto,
> Yr al bihabe*t*.

In the MS. the Scandinavian Runic characters are found. In addition : 1. Under *Feu forman* WREA in English Runic letters and T with one stroke as in *v.* 9. 7. Above Hagal an English H with two crossbars. 8. Above *Ar* an English A. 9. Above *Man* an English M. 11. Above *Yr* a variety of English Y.

THE HEROIC POEMS

Res gestae regumque ducumque et tristia bella
HORACE

INTRODUCTION

WALDHERE

In the year 1860 Professor E. C. Werlauff of the Royal Library, Copenhagen, was looking through some odds and ends of parchment brought back from England by the Icelandic scholar Grímur J. Thorkelin, the first editor of Beowulf, when he came upon two leaves of Anglo-Saxon MS. which had evidently been used in the binding of a book. Upon examination they proved to contain fragments of the Waltharius story, hitherto unknown from English sources, and in the same year Professor George Stephens brought out the *editio princeps* styled *Two Leaves of King Waldere's Lay*.

It was a popular story on the continent and several versions of it are preserved; cf. especially Learned, *The Saga of Walther of Aquitaine* (Baltimore, 1892), and Althof, *Waltharii Poesis*, I. 17–23 (Leipzig, 1899).

1. By far the most complete, as also the earliest, of the continental forms is the Latin epic of Waltharius by Ekkehard of St Gall, the first of that name, ob. 973. It is a poem of 1456 hexameter lines, composed according to a later namesake of the author (usually known as Ekkehard IV) as an academic exercise in the Vergilian mood, *dictamen magistro debitum*. An occasional phrase or turn of syntax betrays its Teutonic origin; cf. Althof, *W. P.* I. 28–32, 44–57, etc.: and Ker, *The Dark Ages*, pp. 222 ff. (Edinburgh, 1904).

Briefly summarised, the story runs as follows: At the time of the great Hunnish invasions there ruled in Gaul three princes of Teutonic blood: (1) Gibicho, king of the Franks, at Worms; his son was called Guntharius. (2) Here-

ricus, king of the Burgundians, at Châlon-sur-Saône; his
daughter Hiltgunt was betrothed to Waltharius, son of (3)
Alpharius, king of Aquitaine. Attacked by a countless
army of the Huns, they could not but submit and render
hostages to Attila. In place of Guntharius, who was then
too young, Gibicho sent Hagano of Trojan blood; but the
others were forced to deliver up their own children. The
hostages were well treated by Attila and raised to high
positions at the Hunnish court. But on the death of Gibicho
Guntharius revolted and Hagano fled to Worms. Thereupon
Attila, fearing lest Waltharius should follow the example
of his sworn companion, proposed to wed him to a Hunnish
maiden. Waltharius, however, induced him to withdraw
the proposition and prepared for flight with Hiltgunt. One
night while the Huns were heavy with wine, they slipped
away, carrying much treasure with them. They fled by
devious ways and all went well till after they had crossed
the Rhine by Worms. Now at last they felt out of danger;
but Guntharius had heard of their arrival and thought only
of recovering the tribute paid by his father to the Huns.
Hagano tried to turn him from so discreditable and dangerous
a venture; but Guntharius would not be gainsaid. With
twelve chosen warriors, of whom the unwilling Hagano was
one, he fell upon Waltharius, who was resting in a defile of
the Vosges. He demanded the treasure and the maiden,
and Waltharius, when his offer first of 100, then 200 rings
had been refused, made a stubborn resistance. The position
was impregnable; eight of the Franks he slew in single
combat and, when the three survivors attacked him with a
trident, he was equally successful. Guntharius and Hagano
then drew off; on the following day Waltharius, who had
left his strong position, was waylaid by them and a furious
combat ensued, in which Guntharius lost a leg, Hagano
an eye and Waltharius his right hand[1].

> *Sic, sic, armillas partiti sunt Avarenses.* (v. 1404)

---

[1] Hence the lords of Wasgenstein,—some ten miles as the crow flies
from Worms—the traditional site of the battle, bore as their coat of arms
six white hands on a red field ; cf. the seal of Johann von Wasichenstein
(1339), figured by Althof, *Das Waltharilied*, pp. 216 ff.

After a formal reconciliation the Franks returned to Worms and Waltharius at length reached home where, after his marriage to Hiltgunt and his father's death, he ruled successfully for thirty years.

2. Waltharius is paraphrased in part in the Italian Chronicon Novaliciense, II. cc. 7–13 (cf. Bethmann, *MGH. ss.* VII. 73–133), where however the story is attached to a local hero, a champion of the Lombard king Desiderius (757–774).

3. There are moreover a few strophes extant of a Bavarian-Austrian epic of the first part of the thirteenth century, which give a somewhat less sanguinary version of the story.

The exceedingly dilapidated fragment from Graz (cf. Müllenhoff, *ZfdA.* XII. 280 ff.) tells how Walther learned for the first time from Hagen, who was on the point of departure from the Hunnish court, that he had been betrothed to Hiltgund; cf. Heinzel, *Die Walthersage*, pp. 13 ff. (Wien, 1888).

A somewhat longer fragment, 39 strophes, is preserved in two MS. leaves from Vienna (cf. Massman, *ZfdA.* II. 216 ff.).

(*a*) After leaving Worms Walther and Hiltgund are escorted home to Langres by Volker and sixty of Gunther's knights. A messenger is sent ahead to Walther's father Alker (or Alpker), who, overjoyed at the news, prepares for their reception.

(*b*) *Hildigunde Brûte* describes Hiltgund's life at Langres, Walther's passionate love and the preparations for the wedding, to which even Etzel (Attila) and his wife are invited.

4. There are numerous incidental references in the Nibelungenlied
(str. 2281,

Nu wer was der ûfem schilde   vor dem Wasgensteine saz,
Dô im von Spâne Walther   sô vil der mâge sluoc.
Str. 1694,
Er und von Spâne Walther ;   die wuohsen hie ze man,
Hagen sand ich wider heim: Walther mit Hiltegunte entran)
and other Middle High German sources; cf. Althof, *Das Waltharilied*, pp. 180–9.

5. In the Þiðriks saga af Bern, cc. 241–4 (Bertelsen, II. 105 ff.), a thirteenth century Norwegian compilation from North German ballads, the story is simplified; Gunther has disappeared and Hǫgni is an agent of the Hunnish king.

Valtari af Vaskasteini, nephew of Erminrikr, king of Apulia, and Hildigund, daughter of Ilias of Greece, hostages to Attila, flee by night from the Hunnish court, taking with them a vast treasure. Pursued by Hǫgni and eleven knights, Valtari turns to bay, kills the eleven Huns and puts Hǫgni to flight. But as Valtari and Hildigund are feasting after the battle, Hǫgni returns to the attack; whereupon Valtari strikes him with the backbone of the boar which he is eating. Hǫgni escapes with the loss of an eye and the fugitives make their way to Erminrik's court without more ado.

6. There is moreover a Polish version of the story, the earliest form of which is to be found in the Chronicon Poloniae by Boguphalus II, Bishop of Posen, ob. 1253; cf. Heinzel, *Das Waltharilied*, pp. 28 ff. and Althof, *W. P.* I. 17–23.

Here Wdaly Walczerz (Walter the Strong) is a Polish count who carries off Helgunda, a Frankish princess, whose love he has won by nightly serenades. At the Rhone he is overtaken by the betrothed of the princess, who challenges him to battle. The pursuer is slain and Walczerz carries home his bride to Tynecz by Cracow. The sequel, which relates how Walczerz is betrayed by Helgunda, cast into prison and helped in the end to vengeance by the sister of his gaoler, has nothing to do with the original story.

It has been suggested that the version found in Þiðriks saga represents the original form of the story. This is most improbable; for while Guthhere appears in Waldhere, by at least two centuries the earliest in point of date, the episode in Þiðriks saga has gone through the ballad process of simplification. It is unfortunate that so little remains of Waldhere; but it may be assumed that in general outlines it followed the story of Waltharius. It varied of course in detail; the characterisation of the heroine is vastly different. Contrast with Waldhere A the corresponding passages of Waltharius:

v. 544: *In terramque cadens effatur talia tristis:*

"*Obsecro, mi senior, gladio mea colla secentur,*

"*Ut quae non merui pacto thalamo sociari*

"*Nullius alterius patiar consortia carnis*";

v. 1213: "*Dilatus jam finis adest; fuge domne propinquant;* and Þiðriks saga, c. 243: *Herra, harmr er þat, er þu skallt .i. beriaz við .xij. riddara. Rið hœlldr aptr oc forðu þinu liui.* Nor is it likely that the grotesque ending of Waltharius found a place in the English version. Moreover it appears that Waldhere encountered first Hagena, then Guthhere, whereas Guntharius and Hagano made a combined attack upon Waltharius.

It may be advisable to say something on the historical bearings of the story, discussed at length by Heinzel, Althof, and Clarke, *Sidelights on Teutonic History in the Migration Period,* pp. 209–231.

Aetla (Attila) is of course the great king of the Huns ob. 453, the *flagella Dei,* who terrorised Europe for some twenty years until defeated by Aetius on the Catalaunian plains; cf. Chambers, *Widsith,* pp. 44–48.

Guthhere (the Gunnarr—Gunther of the Old Norse and Middle High German Nibelung cycles) is the historical king of the Burgundians, who in the year 411 set up the Emperor Jovinus and, as a reward for surrendering his puppet, was allowed to occupy the left bank of the Rhine. For twenty years he ruled at Worms: then, perhaps under pressure from the Huns, he invaded Belgic Gaul and was thrown back by Aetius (435). Two years later he was defeated and slain by the Huns, and the sorry remnants of his people took refuge in the modern Burgundy. He is the Gundaharius of the Lex Burgundionum issued by his successor Gundobad in 516; cf. Chambers, *Widsith,* pp. 60–63.

In Waltharius however he is represented as a Frank, Hiltgunt and Herericus as Burgundians; for, since in the tenth century Worms was Frankish, Chalon-sur-Saône Burgundian, Ekkehard applied the political geography o his own time to a story of the migration period. It is quite uncertain therefore of what nationality these persons really were. Learned suggests that Herericus may be a reminiscence of the Chararicus who ruled Burgundy after the Frankish conquest (Gregory of Tours, IV. 38). But as in the case of Waltharius himself, nothing definite is known.

In the Anglo-Saxon fragments Waldhere is simply called 'the son of Aelfhere'—the Alpharius of Ekkehard, *v.* 77. Hence it has been thought that, as Aquitaine was held by the Visigoths in the days of Attila, the hero belonged to that people—a view most probably held in the later Middle Ages; e.g. he is called *Walther von Spanje*, Walter of Spain, in the Nibelungenlied. But it is likely that the original story had some native name, which has been displaced by the classical 'Aquitania.' Now the battle between Waldhere and his foes took place in the Vosges (*Vosegus*, Ekkehard passim: *vor dem Vasgensteine*, Nibelungenlied, 2281), whence he is styled *Valtari af Vaskasteini* in þiðriks saga; and so before the time of Ekkehard the name of the Vosges must have been confused with *Vasconia = Aquitania*; cf. the "Wessobrunner Gloss" of the eighth century: *Equitania: uuasconolant*[1].

A different indication is furnished by the MHG. fragments: there too he is called *der vogt von Spânje*, but his home is placed at *Lengers*, the French Langres (dept Haute-Marne), no very great distance from Chalon-sur-Saône, the home of Hiltgunt in Ekkehard, *v.* 52. Of course the Merovingian conquest of Gaul had hardly begun as yet; but it is not at all unlikely that there were small Teutonic communities to the S.W. of the Vosges already in the first half of the fifth century. For certain Teutonic place-names in that district confirm the statement of Eumenius that Constantius Chlorus settled "barbarian cultivators" in the neighbourhood of Langres; cf. Chadwick, *Heroic Age*, p. 162; Zeuss, *Die Deutschen und die Nachbarstämme*, pp. 336, 582–4. Waldhere may or may not have belonged

[1] Cf. *P.G.*₍₂₎ III. 707.

to one of these communities: this much at least is certain that, like Sigurd and other heroes of the migration period, he was a character of no historical importance.

FINN.

The Finn fragment, incomplete at the beginning and the end, was discovered in the Lambeth Palace Library towards the end of the seventeenth century. The MS. has since been lost; luckily it had been printed in *Linguarum Veterum Septentrionalium Thesaurus*, I. 192 ff. (London, 1705), the monumental work of Dr George Hickes, the non-juring Dean of Worcester and one of the most devoted of those eighteenth century scholars to whom we owe so much.

The story of Finn must have been popular in Anglo-Saxon times. It is the subject of an episode in Beowulf, *vv.* 1068–1159, and three at least of its characters are included in the epic catalogue of Widsith:

 v. 27. *Finn Folcwalding (weold) Fresna cynne;*

 v. 29. *Hnæf Hocingum;*

 v. 31. *Sæferð Sycgum.*

Moreover the *Finn filii Fodepald*—Nennius Interpretatus, *Finn (filii Frenn), filii Folcvald*[1]—who appears as an ancestor of Hengest in *Historia Brittonum*, § 31, a mistake for the *Finn Godwulfing* of other Anglo-Saxon texts (e.g. Chronicle 547 A), is clearly due to acquaintance with the story of Finn, the son of Folcwald[2].

From the continent evidence is scanty; the name Nebi (Hnæf) is occasionally found in Alemannic charters and Thegan, *Vita Ludovici*, c. II., gives the following as the genealogy of Hildegard, the wife of Charlemagne: *Godefridus dux genuit Huochingum, Huochingus genuit Nebi, Nebi genuit Immam, Imma uero Hiltigardam*; cf. Müllenhoff, *ZfdA*. XI. 282.

From Beowulf, *v.* 1068–1159, it appears that Hnaef, a vassal prince of the Danes, met his death among the Frisians at the court of Finn. The reasons for his presence there are

[1] Mommsen, *Chronica Minora*, p. 171 (Berlin, 1898).
[2] Chadwick, *Origin of the English Nation*, p. 42.

nowhere stated in the episode or in the fragment. Very
probably they were connected by marriage; the episode at
least suggests that Hildeburh, described as *Hoces dohtor* in
v. 1076, was the wife of Finn. She may have been Hnaef's
sister, since in Widsith, v. 29, Hnaef is said to have ruled
the Hocingas, and this would agree with *v.* 1074, where
Hildeburh bewails the loss of sons and brothers, perhaps
a poetical use of plural for singular; cf. *vv.* 1114–1117.
Hnaef's followers, led by a certain Hengest, hold out in the
palace-hall and inflict such fearful loss upon the Frisians
that Finn is forced to come to terms. An agreement is
made—in flat defiance of the spirit of the *comitatus*—and
peace is kept throughout the winter. But when spring
returns, Oslaf and Guthlaf, two of Hnaef's retainers (cf.
Ordlaf and Guþlaf of Finn *v.* 18) make their way home.
Determined to avenge their fallen lord, they collect rein-
forcements and return to Friesland, where they wipe out
their dishonour in the blood of Finn and all his followers.

The story opens with the fall of Hnaef; nothing is known
of its antecedents. The elaborate superstructure reared
by Müllenhoff (*Nordalbingische Studien*, I. 157) and Simrock
(*Beowulf*, p. 190 ff.)—the death of Folcwald at the hands of
Hoc, the settlement of the blood-feud by the marriage of
Finn and Hildeburh, the subsequent murder of Hnaef while
on a visit to the Frisian court—is pure hypothesis, erected
on analogy with the *Ingeld* story; cf. Beowulf, *vv.* 2020–2066
and Saxo, Book VI. There is no reason for ascribing treachery
to Finn—*Eotena treowe* (Beow. *v.* 1071) refers to the loyalty
of Hnaef's men, not to the bad faith of the Frisians—and it
is just as probable that Hnaef was the aggressor.

The episode in Beowulf is to be regarded as a paraphrase
of some full-length treatment of the subject; cf. Odyssey VIII.
499 and the cyclic poem of the Sack of Troy ('Ιλίου Πέρcιc)[1].
But it is not easy to square the fragment with it. On the
whole it seems most reasonable to assume that the fragment
opens after the death of Hnaef, describes the battle hinted

[1] D. B. Monro, *Homer's Odyssey, Books XIII–XXIV*, pp. 371 ff. Oxford,
1901).

at in Beowulf and breaks off just before the armistice of
v. 1085. The *hearogeong cyning* would then be Hengest,
the *folces hyrde* Finn. It is true that in Beowulf, *v.* 1085,
Hengest is styled *þeodnes ðegne*, an epithet scarcely com-
patible with *hearogeong cyning*, since in Anglo-Saxon epic
poetry the title *cyning* is confined to ruling princes. Moreover it would seem from Finn, *v.* 43, that there had been
at least five days fighting, whereas in Beowulf the battle
was over in a single night. These difficulties have given rise
to divergent views as to the precise moment in the story to
which the fragment relates; Möller (*Altenglische Volksepos*,
p. 65) places it between *vv.* 1143–4 of Beowulf, Bugge
(*P.B.B.* XII. 20 ff.), before the death of Hnaef. But the
balance of probability is in favour of the view expressed
above[1].

DEOR.

The MS. of Deor is to be found on fol. 100 of the Exeter
Book, the *mycel Englisc boc be gehwylcum þingum on Leod-
wisan geworht*, presented to Exeter by Bishop Leofric (1050–
1072), and still preserved in the Cathedral Library there.

Setting aside *vv.* 23–34, the poem consists of six short
strophes of irregular length followed by a refrain. Each of
the first five strophes recounts some dolorous episode from
heroic story, Weland's captivity at the hands of Nithhad, the
Geat's hopeless love for Maethhild, the thirty years of exile
suffered by Theodric, the sixth the poet's own misfortunes.
The form is almost unique in Anglo-Saxon poetry, the only
other instance being the so-called First Riddle of Cynewulf
with its refrain *ungelic is us*. It is usually styled Deor's
Lament (des Sängers Trost) and reckoned among the lyrics,
but the only passage which recalls the Wanderer and the

---

[1] In a paper read before the Philological Society on Dec. 6th, 1912,
Dr R. W. Chambers has suggested that the fight was a three-cornered affair.
Hnaef of the Healf-Dene and Garulf of the Eotenas came to blows at
a meeting of princes. Hnaef was slain and Finn stepped in to end the
battle, afterwards taking Hengest into his service. An outline of the argu-
ment is given in no. 4442 of the *Athenaeum* and on pp. 168–9 of his edition
of Wyatt's *Beowulf* (Cambridge, 1914). In the meantime we are awaiting
his promised *Introduction to the Study of Beowulf.*

Seafarer, the Husband's Message and the Wife's Complaint, is *vv.* 28–34, which is generally recognised to be a late homiletic addition. Deor has lost his all, but the prevailing note is hope rather than despair. The refrain seems conclusive on that point; Weland wreaked vengeance on his oppressor, Beadohild brought forth a mighty son, Theodric won back his kingdom, the cruel Eormanric died a bloody death. Their troubles were surmounted, so may Deor's be. With Lawrence (*Mod. Phil.* IX. 23), rather may we call the poem a veritable *Consolatio Philosophiae* of minstrelsy.

HILDEBRAND.

The fragment of the *Hildebrandeslied*, the only surviving relic of German heroic poetry, was found on the outer cover of a theological MS.—No. 56 in the *Landesbibliothek* at Kassel. This MS. was written in the early part of the ninth century, and from a palaeographical point of view has considerable traces of Anglo-Saxon influence. Fulda was probably its home[1]; but the variations presented as well in language as orthography are so great that it cannot be classified as a specimen of any known dialect. High German and Low German forms are found side by side, even in the same word.

A convenient table of the dialectical peculiarities has been given by Mansion in his *Ahd. Lesebuch*, p. 113 ff. (Heidelberg, 1912), from which the following particulars are taken:

Consonants.

1.   Original *p* and *t* remain as in Old Saxon; cf.
    v. 88 *werpan*, 62 *scarpen*.
    v. 16 *heittu*, 27 *ti*, 52 *đat*.

2.   Orig. *k* becomes *ch* initially and after consonants as in O.H.G.; cf. *v.* 28 *chud*, 10 *folche* etc.:
    elsewhere it is represented indifferently by *k*, *h*, *ch*; cf.
    v. 1 *ik*, 17 *ih*, 13 *chunincriche*.

---

[1] *Hiltibraht* for *Hiltibrant* is paralleled in other documents from Fulda; cf. Kauffmann, *Festgabe für Sievers*, p. 136 ff. (Leipzig, 1896) and Kögel, *P.G.*, II. 74.

3. Orig. *đ* becomes regularly *t* as in O.H.G.;
   cf. *v.* 35 *truhtin*, 44 *tot*.
4. Orig. *đ*, when final, becomes *p*: cf. *v.* 27 *leop*, *v.* 34 *gap*;
   in other positions we find *b*: cf. *v.* 30 *obana*, etc.
   (*pist, prut, sippan, hevane* are exceptions.)
5. Orig. *ʒ* regularly becomes *g* (*v.* 37 *geru* etc.), except
   when final, where we find *c*; cf. *v.* 43 *wic*, 55 *taoc*.
6. Orig. *þ* normally becomes *d*; but cf. *v.* 3 *Hađubrant*.
7. *n* disappears before *þ, s*, as in Anglo-Frisian and generally in the Heliand; cf. *v.* 5 *guđhamun*, 12 *odre*,
   15 *usere*.
8. Erratic use of *h*; cf. *v.* 6 *ringa* (*hringa*), 57 *bihrahanan*
   (*birahanan*).

Vowels.

1. Orig. *ō* is represented indifferently by *o* and *uo*: cf.
   v. 8 *frotoro*, 11 *cnuosles*.
2. Orig. *ē* is represented by *ae* and *ę*: cf. *v.* 19 *furlaet*,
   61 *lęttun*.
3. Orig. *au* (O.H.G. *ou*) is represented by *au* and *ao*: cf.
   v. 55 *rauba*. 53 *taoc*; sometimes also by *o* in cases
   where O.H.G. has *ō*; cf. *v.* 1 *gihorta*, 18 *floh*; but on
   the other hand *ao* appears in *v.* 22 *laosa*, 55 *aodlihho*.
4. Orig. *ai* is represented in a variety of ways:
   ai, v. 65 *staimbort*?; *ei, v.* 17 *heittu*; *œ, v.* 17 *hœtti*;
   ae, v. 22 *raet*; *e, v.* 47 *heme*; *ę, v.* 52 *ęnigeru*.

Perhaps the most satisfactory solution of the problem is
that put forward by Francis A. Wood, *P.M.L.A.* XI. 323–330,
who argues that in its present form the Hildebrandeslied
goes back to an Old Saxon poem current in the eighth
century; heard from the lips of a Low German minstrel, it
was written down in High German orthography and written
down from memory, as is shown by the frequent deviations into
prose. The existing MS. is not the archetype, but a copy of
the original; the meaningless repetition of *darba gistontun*
after *v.* 26 seems conclusive on this point[1].

[1] The exact converse of this view is vigorously expressed by Holtzmann,
Germania, IX. 289 ff. and Luft, *Festgabe an K. Weinhold*, pp. 27 ff. (Leipzig,

The hero of the poem is that Hildebrand who occupies a far from insignificant position in the Nibelungenlied and the poems of the Heldenbuch. The story of the fragment, unknown from either of these sources, is concerned with the meeting of Hildebrand and his son Hadubrand. Leaving his wife and child at home Hildebrand has followed Dietrich to the court of Etzel, and now returning after thirty years of exile finds his son arrayed against him. He learns their kinship and reveals himself; but Hadubrand, suspecting treachery, refuses to believe him. The fragment breaks off just as the fight begins; but there can be no doubt that as in the Sohrab and Rustum story from the Shah-Nameh the father is obliged to slay his son[2].

The whole atmosphere of the fragment forebodes a tragic sequel, though it is true that later German poems on the subject, as well as the closely related episode in Þiðriks saga, cc. 405–409 (Bertelsen, II. 471; also in Holthausen's *Altisländisches Lesebuch*, p. 24 ff.), end happily with the mutual recognition of the father and the son. Such are:—

1. The fifteenth century *Der vater mit dem sun*, of Kaspar von der Rön; cf. Henrici, *Das deutsche Heldenbuch*, pp. 301 ff., translated by F. A. Wood, *The Hildebrandslied*, pp. 7 ff. (Chicago, 1914).

2. A broadsheet of 1515; cf. von Liliencron, *Deutsches Leben im Volkslied um* 1530, pp. 84 ff.

Moreover an allusion to the death of Hadubrand is preserved in a poem found both in Saxo Book VII. (Holder, p. 244):

> *medioxima nati*
> *Illita conspicuo species caelamine constat*
> *Cui manus haec cursum metae vitalis ademit.*
> *Unicus hic nobis haeres erat, una paterni*
> *Cura animi, superoque datus solamine matri.*
> *Sors mala, quae laetis infaustos aggerit annos,*
> *Et risum maerore premit sortemque molestat,*

1896); for the literature of the subject, cf. Braune, *Ahd. Lesebuch*[7], p. 188 (Halle, 1911).

[2] A comparative study of the motive will be found in M. A. Potter, *Sohrab and Rustem* (London, 1899).

and in Ásmundarsaga Kappabana, c. IX. (*Fornaldar Sögur,*
III. 355):

> *Liggr þar inn svási   sonr at höfði*
> *eptirerfingi,   er ek eiga gat,*
> *oviljandi   aldrs synjaðak.*

There is one reference to Hildebrand in early English
literature in the thirteenth century fragment, discovered in
Peterhouse Library by the Provost of King's:

> *Ita quod dicere possunt cum Wade:*
> *Summe sende ylues*
> *and summe sende nadderes;*
> *summe sende nikeres*
> *the bi den watere* (MS. *biden patez*) *wunien.*
> *Nister man nenne*
> *bute Ildebrand onne*[1].

These six lines are perhaps to be connected with the M.H.G.
poem Virginal; see p. 60.

---

[1] Cf. *Academy*, Feb. 1896, No. 1241; *Athenaeum*, Feb. 1896, No. 3565.

BIBLIOGRAPHY OF THE HEROIC POEMS.

WALDHERE.

Editions (with translation*).

*Stephens, G. *Two Leaves of King Waldere's Lay.* Copenhagen, 1860.
Müllenhoff, K. and Dietrich. *ZfdA.* XII. 264 ff., XXX. 259 ff.
Rieger, M. *Alt.- u. Angelsächs. Lesebuch,* pp. xviij ff. Giessen, 1861.
*Haigh, D. H. *Anglo-Saxon Sagas,* pp. 125 ff. London, 1861.
Grein, C. W. M. *Beowulf nebst den Fragm. Finnsburg u. Waldere,* pp. 76 ff. Cassel u. Göttingen, 1867.
Weinhold, K., in Scheffel and Holder's *Waltharius,* pp. 168 ff. Stuttgart, 1874.
Wülker, R. P. *Kleinere ags. Dichtungen,* pp. 8 ff. Leipzig, 1879.
Grein-Wülker. *Bibl. der ags. Poesie,* I. 7 ff., 401 ff. Kassel, 1881–3.
Möller, H. *Das ae. Volksepos,* pp. lxxvj ff. Kiel, 1883.
Heinzel, R. *Die Walthersage.* Wien, 1888.
Kluge, F. *Ags. Lesebuch(3),* pp. 128 ff. Halle, 1902.
Holthausen, Ferd. *Die ae. Walderebruchstücke,* with four autotypes (*Göteborgs Högskolas Årskrift,* 1899).
Trautmann, M. *B.B.* v. 162 ff.; XVI. 184 ff.
Strecker, K. *Ekkehards Waltharius,* pp. 94 ff. Berlin, 1907.
Fraatz, P. *Darstellung der syntakt. Erscheinungen in den ags. Waldere Bruchstücken,* pp. 7 ff. Rostock dissert., 1908.
Holthausen, F. *Beowulf nebst den kleineren Denkmälern der Heldensage(3).* Heidelberg, 1912–3.
Sedgefield, W. J. *Beowulf(2),* pp. 105 ff. Manchester, 1913.

English Translations.

(For German etc., *see* Holthausen, op. cit.)
Gummere, F. B. *The Oldest English Epic,* pp. 167 ff. New York, 1909.
Clarke, M. G. *Sidelights on Teutonic History during the Migration Period,* pp. 219 ff. Cambridge, 1911.

Commentaries.

Bugge, S. *Spredte iagttagelser* (*Tidskrift,* VIII. 72 ff., 305 ff.).
Kölbing, E. *Die W.-Fragmente* (*E. St.* v. 240 ff., 292 ff.).
Möller, H. *Das ae. Volksepos,* pp. 156 ff. Kiel, 1883.

Müller, W. *Zur Mythologie der deutschen Heldensage*, pp. 11 ff. Heilbronn, 1886.

Dieter, F. *Die Walderefragmente und die ursp. Gestalt der Walthersage* (*Anglia*, x. 227 ff., xi. 159 ff.).

Symons, B. *P.G.*(2), iii. 793 ff.

Kögel, R. *P.G.*(2), ii. 81 ff.

—— *Geschichte der deutschen Litteratur*, i. 1. 275 ff. Strassburg, 1894.

Learned, M. D. *The Saga of Walther of Aquitaine*. Baltimore, 1892.

Cosign, P. J. *De Waldere-Fragmenten (Verslagen en mededeelingen d. k. akad. van Wetensch.*, iii. reeks, xii.). Amsterdam, 1895.

Binz, G. *Zeugnisse zur germ. Sage in England* (*P.B.B.* xii. 217 ff.).

Althof, H. *Über einige Stellen im Waltharius u. die ags. Waldere-Fragmente*. Weimar Programm. 1899.

—— *Waltharii Poesis*. Leipzig, 1899–1905.

—— *Das Waltharilied*. Leipzig, 1902.

—— *Über einige Namen im Waltharius* (*ZfdPh.* xxxiv. 365 ff.).

Trautmann, M. *B.B.* xi. 135 ff.

Brandl, A. *P.G.*(2), ii. 986 ff.

Boer, R. C. *Unterss. über die Hildesage* (*ZfdPh.* xi. 1 ff.).

Roethe, G. *Nibelungias u. Waltharius* (*Sitzb. der Berl. Akad.* 1909, xxv. 649 ff.).

Eckerth, W. *Das Waltherlied*(2). Halle, 1909.

Dröge, K. *Nibelungenlied u. Waltharius* (*ZfdA.* lii. 193 ff.).

Clarke, M. G. *Sidelights*, pp. 209 ff.

Chadwick, H. M. *The Heroic Age*, passim. Cambridge, 1912.

THE FINN FRAGMENT.

Editions (with translation*).

Hickes, G. *Linguarum Veterum Septentrionalium Thesaurus*, i. 192 ff. Oxford, 1705.

*Conybeare, J. J. *The British Bibliographer*, iv. 261 ff. London, 1814.

* —— *Illustrations of Anglo-Saxon Poetry*, pp. 175 ff. London, 1826.

Grundtvig, S. *Bjovulfs Drape*, pp. xl ff. Köbenhavn, 1820.

Kemble, J. M. *Beowulf*(2), i. 238 ff. London, 1835.

Klipstein, L. *Analecta Anglo-Saxonica*, i. 426 ff. New York, 1849.

Ettmüller, L. *Engla and Seaxna Scopas and Boceras*, pp. 130 ff. Quedlinburg, 1850.

*Thorpe, B. *Beowulf*, pp. 227 ff. Oxford, 1855 and 1875.

Grein, C. W. M. *Bibl. d. ags. Poesie*, i. 341 ff. Göttingen, 1857.

Grundtvig, S. *Beowulfes Beorh*, pp. 37 ff. Köbenhavn, 1861.

Rieger, M. *Ags. Lesebuch*, pp. 61 ff. Giessen, 1861.

Wülker, R. P.   *Kleinere ags. Dichtungen*, pp. 6 ff.   Leipzig, 1879.
Grein-Wülker.   *Bibl. d. ags. Poesie*, I. 14 ff.   Kassel, 1881.
Möller, H.   *Das ae. Volksepos*, II. vij ff.   Kiel, 1883.
Kluge, F.   *Ags. Lesebuch*(3), pp. 127 ff.   Halle, 1902.
Trautmann, M.   *Finn u. Hildebrand* (*B.B.* VII. 54 ff.).   Bonn, 1903.
—— *Beowulf* (*B.B.* XVI. 180 ff.).   Bonn, 1904.
Heyne, M.—Schücking, L. L.   *Beowulf* (9), pp. 91 ff.   Paderborn, 1910.
Sedgefield, W. J.   *Beowulf* (2), pp. 99 ff.   Manchester, 1913.
Holthausen, F.   *Beowulf* (3).   Heidelberg, 1912–13.
Wyatt, A. J.—Chambers, R. W.   *Beowulf with the Finnsburg Fragment*, pp. 158 ff.   Cambridge, 1914.

English Translations.

(For German etc., *see* Holthausen, op. cit.)

Haigh, D. H.   *Anglo-Saxon Sagas*, pp. 32 ff.   London, 1861.
Brooke, Stopford A.   *History of Early English Literature*, I. 88 ff.   London, 1892.
Garnett, J. M.   *Beowulf* (4), pp. 97 ff.   Boston, 1900.
Child, C. G.   *Beowulf and the Finnesburh Fragment*, pp. 89 ff.   London, 1904.
Huyshe, W.   *Beowulf: An Old English Epic*, pp. 200 ff.   London, 1907.
Gummere, F. B.   *The Oldest English Epic*, pp. 160 ff.   New York, 1909.
Clark Hall, J. R.   *Beowulf and the Finnsburg Fragment* (2), pp. 156 ff.   London, 1911.

Commentaries.

Ettmüller, L.   *Beowulf*, pp. 36 ff.   Zürich, 1840.
Uhland, L.   *Schriften zur Gesch. der Dichtung u. Sage*, VIII. 488 ff. (from *Germ.* II. 354 ff.).
Müllenhoff, K.   *Zur Kritik des ags. Volksepos* (*ZfdA.* XI. 281 ff.).
—— *Nordalbingische Studien*, I. 156 ff.   Kiel, 1844.
Simrock, K.   *Beowulf*, pp. 187 ff.   Stuttgart u. Augsburg, 1859.
Haigh, D. H.   *Anglo-Saxon Sagas*, pp. 29 ff.
Grein, C. W. M.   *Die hist. Verhältn. des Beowulfliedes* (*Eberts Jahrbuch*, IV. 269 ff.).
Holtzmann, A.   *Zu Beowulf* (*Germ.* VIII. 474 ff.).
Grein, C. W. M.   *Zur Textkritik der ags. Dichter* (*Germ.* X. 422).
Bugge, S.   *Spredte iagttagelser* (*Tidskrift*, VIII. 304 ff.).
Dederich, H.   *Historische u. geographische Studien zum Beowulfliede*, pp. 215 ff.   Köln, 1877.
Möller, H.   *Das ae. Volksepos*, I. 46 ff., 151 ff.   Kiel, 1883.
ten Brink, B.   *P.G.* (1), II. 1. 545 ff.   Strassburg, 1893.

Schilling, H.   *Notes on the Finnsaga* (*M.L.N.* I. 89 ff., 116 ff.).
—— *The Finnsburg Fragment and the Finn Episode* (*M.L.N.* II. 146 ff.).
Bugge, S.   *Das Finnsburg-Fragment* (*P.B.B.* XII. 20 ff.).
Jellinek, M. H.   *Zum Finnsburgfragment* (*P.B.B.* XV. 428 ff.).
Clark Hall, J. R.   *Beowulf*(2), pp. 202 ff.
Binz, G.   *P.B.B.* XX. 179 ff.
Boer, R. C.   *Finnsage u. Nibelungensage* (*ZfdA.* XLVII. 125 ff., 139 ff.).
Holthausen, F.   *Beiträge zur Erklärung des ae. Epos* (*ZfdPh.* XXVII. 123 ff.).
Klaeber, Fr.   *Anglia*, XXVIII. 447.
—— *Archiv f. n. S.* CXV. 181 ff.
Swiggett, G. L.   *Notes on the Finnsburg Fragment* (*M.L.N.* XX. 169 ff.).
Rieger, M.   *Zum Kampf in Finnsburg* (*ZfdA.* XLVIII. 9 ff.).
Klaeber, F.   *Zum Finnsburg-Kampfe* (*E. St.* XXXIX. 307 ff.).
Brandl, A.   *P.G.*(2) II. 983 ff.
Clarke, M. G.   *Sidelights on Teutonic History*, pp. 177 ff.
Wyatt-Chambers.   *Beowulf*, pp. 167 ff.

DEOR.

Editions (with translation *)

*Conybeare, J. J.   *Illustrations of A.-S. Poetry*, pp. 240 ff.   London, 1826.
Grimm, W. K.   *Deutsche Heldensage*(3), p. 22.   Gütersloh, 1889.
*Thorpe, B.   *Codex Exoniensis*, pp. 377 ff.   London, 1842.
Klipstein, L.   *Analecta Anglo-Saxonica*, II. 317 ff.
Ettmüller, L.   *Engla and Seaxna Scopas*, pp. 211 ff.
Müller, Th.   *Ags. Lesebuch*, pp. 171 ff.   (1855 ?)
Rieger, M.   *Ags. Lesebuch*, pp. 82 ff.
Grein-Wülker.   *Bibl. der ags. Poesie*, I. 283 ff.
Kluge, F.   *Ags. Lesebuch*(3), pp. 139 ff.
Sedgefield, W. J.   *Beowulf*(2), pp. 107 ff.
Holthausen, F.   *Beowulf*(3).

English Translations.

Haigh, D. H.   *A.-S. Sagas*, pp. 102 ff.
—— *Atlantic Monthly*, LXVII. 287.   Boston and New York, 1891.
Gummere, F. B.   *The Oldest English Epic*, pp. 185 ff.

Commentaries.

Müllenhoff, K.   *ZfdA.* VII. 530 ff.; XI. 272 ff.; XII. 261.
Grein, C. W. M.   *Germ.* X. 422.
Meyer, K.   *Germ.* XIV. 283 ff.
—— *Die Dietrichsage.*   Basel, 1868.
Schipper, J.   *Germ.* XIX. 333.

54   *Bibliography*

Möller, H. *Das ae. Volksepos*, I. 115 ff.
Morley, H. *English Writers*(2), II. 15 ff. London, 1888.
Golther, W. *Die Wielandsage* (*Germ.* XXXIII. 449 ff.).
Heinzel, R. *Über die ostgotische Heldensage*, pp. 16 ff. Wien, 1889.
ten Brink, B. *Early English Literature*, pp. 60 ff. London, 1891.
Jiriczek, O. L. *Deutsche Heldensagen*, I. pp. 124 ff., 157. Strassburg, 1898.
Tupper, F. jun. *Deor's Complaint* (*M.L.N.* X. 125 ff.).
—— *Deor* (*M.Ph.* IX. 265 ff.).
—— *The Third Strophe of Deor* (*Anglia* XXXVII. 118 ff.).
Binz, G. *P.B.B.* XX. 192 ff.
Schücking, L. L. *Das ags. Gedicht von der "Klage der Frau"* (*ZfdA.* XLVIII. 436 ff.).
Bugge, S. *The Norse Lay of Wayland and its Relation to English Tradition* (*Sagabook of the Viking Club*, II. 271 ff.; also in Norwegian in *Ark. f. n. F.* XXVI. 33 ff.).
Schück, H. *Bidrag til tolkning af Rök inskriften* (*Uppsala Univ. Årsskrift*, 1908).
Brandl, A. *P.G.*(2), II. 975 ff.
—— *Zur Gotensage bei den AS.* (*Archiv f. n. S.* CXX. 1 ff.).
Stefanović, S. *Zu Deor*, v. 14–17 (*Anglia*, XXXIII. 397 ff.; XXXVI. 383 ff.; XXXVII. 533 ff.).
Lawrence, W. W. *The Song of Deor* (*Mod. Phil.* IX. 23 ff.).
Chambers, R. W. *Widsith*, pp. 15 ff. Cambridge, 1912.
Clarke, M. G. *Sidelights on Teutonic History*, pp. 118 ff.

HILDEBRAND.

Editions.

v. Eckart, J. G. *Commentarii de rebus Franciae orientalis*, I. 864 ff. Wirceburgi, 1729.
Grimm, Die Brüder. *Das Lied von Hildebrand u. Hadubrand*, etc. Cassel, 1812.
Grimm, W. *De Hildebrando...fragmentum.* Göttingen, 1830.
Vollmer, A.—Hofmann, K. *Das Hildebrandslied.* Leipzig, 1850.
Grein, C. W. M. *Das Hl.* Marburg, 1858; Cassel, 1880.
Sievers, Ed. *Das Hl.*, etc. Halle, 1872.
Wackernagel, W. *Altdeutsches Lesebuch*(5). Basel, 1873.
Heinzel, P. *Über die ostgotische Heldensage*, pp. 39 ff. Wien, 1889.
Müllenhoff, K.—Scherer, W. *Denkmäler deutscher Poesie u. Prosa*(3), I. 2 ff.; II. 8 ff. Berlin, 1892.
Wadstein, E. *Göteborgs Högskolas Årsskrift*, IX. Göteborg, 1903.
Trautmann, M. *Finn u. Hildebrand* (*B. B.* VII.). Bonn, 1903.
v. Grienberger, Th. *Das Hl.* Wien, 1908.

v. d. Leyen, F. *Älteste deutsche Dichtungen.* Leipzig, 1909.
Braune, W. *Althochdeutsches Lesebuch* (7), pp. 80 ff. Halle, 1911.
Mansion, J. *Ahd. Lesebuch,* pp. 113 ff. Heidelberg, 1912.
Holthausen, F. *Beowulf* (3). Heidelberg, 1912–3.

English Translations.

(For German, *see* Braune and Holthausen, op. cit.)

Gummere, F. B. *The Oldest English Epic,* pp. 173 ff. New York, 1909.
Wood, F. A. *The Hildebrandslied.* Chicago, 1914.

Commentaries.

Lachmann, K. *Über das Hildebrandslied* (*Kleinere Schriften,* I. 407 ff.). Berlin, 1876.
Holtzmann, A. *Germania,* IX. 289 ff.
Rieger, M. *Ib.* IX. 295.
Schröder, O. *Bemerkungen zur Hl.* (*Symbolae Joachimicae,* pp. 189 ff.). Berlin, 1880.
Edzardi, A. *P. B. B.,* VIII. 480–90.
Möller, H. *Über ahd. Alliterationspoesie.* Kiel, 1888.
Kögel, R. *P. G.* (2). II. 71 ff.
—— *Geschichte der deutschen Litteratur,* I. 1. 211 ff. Strassburg, 1894.
Luft, W. *Die Entwickelung des Dialoges im alten Hl.* Berlin dissert. 1895.
—— *Zum Dialekt des Hl.* (*Festgabe an K. Weinhold,* pp. 29 ff.). Leipzig, 1896.
Kauffmann, F. *Das Hl.* (*Festgabe für E. Sievers,* pp. 124 ff.). Halle, 1896.
Erdmann, A. *Bemerkungen zum Hl.* (*P.B.B.* XXII. 424 ff.).
Meissner, R. *Zum Hl.* (*ZfdA.* XLII. 122 ff.).
—— *Staimbort chludun* (*ib.* XLVII. 400 ff.).
Joseph, E. *Der Dialog des alten Hl.* (*ib.* XLIII. 59 ff.).
Busse, Br. *Sagengeschichtliches zum Hl.* (*P.B.B.* XXVI. 1 ff.).
Franck, J. *Die Überlieferung des Hl.* (*ZfdA.* XLVII. 1 ff.).
Rieger, M. *Zum Hl.* (*ZfdPh.* XLVIII. 1 ff.).
Ehrismann, G. *Zum Hl.* (*P.B.B.* XXXII. 260 ff.).
Klaeber, F. *Hl.* 63 f. (*M.L.N.* XXI. 110 ff.).
—— *Jottings on the Hl.* (*ib.* XXVI. 211 ff.).
Boer, R. C. *De liederen van H. en Hadubrand.* (*Verslagen d. k. akad. van Wetensch.,* IV. reeks, IX.). Amsterdam, 1909.
Wadstein, E. *Minneskrift utg. af filolog. samfundet,* pp. 86 ff. (also in *G. Högskolas Årskrift,* XVI.). Göteborg, 1910.
Collitz, H. *Zum Hl.* (*P.B.B.* XXXVI. 336 ff.).

WALDHERE

A.

.........hyrde hine georne:

"Huru Welande[*s* *ge*]worc ne geswiceð
monna ænigum, þara ðe Mimming can
hearne gehealdan. Oft æt hilde gedreas

5 swatfag ond sweordwund sec[*g*] æfter oðru*m*.
Ætlan ordwyga, ne læt ðin ellen nu gyt
gedreosan to dæge, dryhtscipe [*feallan*]
.........Nu is se dæg cumen,
þæt ðu scealt aninga oðer twega,

10 lif forleosan, oððe lang*n*e dom
agan mid eldum, Ælfheres sunu.
Nalles ic ðe, wine min, wordu*m* cid[*e*]
[*ðy*] ic ðe gesawe æt ðam sweordplegan
ðurh edwitscype æniges monnes

15 wig forbugan, oððe on weal fleon,
lice beorgan, ðeah þe laðra fela
ðinne byrnhomon billu*m* heowun.

A 2. MS. *Weland...worc.*   5. MS. *sec.*
7. *feallan* supplied by Stephens. 10. MS. *lange.*
13. MS. *sweordwlegan.*

A 1. *hyrde*: probably from *hyrdan* (*heard*), " to encourage "; cf.
Elene, v. 841: *þa wæs hige onhyrded* (Dietrich). It might also come from
hyran, " to hear."
Bugge, however (*Tidskrift*, VIII. 72), regards it as too abrupt an opening
for a speech and refers *hyrde* to the sword Mimming, " carefully (Weland)
tempered it." But Cosijn compares Beowulf, v. 2813: *het hine brucan wel.*
A 2. For the opening of a speech with *huru* cf. Guthlac, v. 332 and
the Address of the Soul to the Body, v. 1:
Huru þæs behofaþ hæleþa æghwylc.
Welande[s ge]worc: cf. Beowulf, v. 454, and Waltharius, v. 964; for the
story of Weland, Beadohild, Niðhad and Widia see notes to Deor, pp. 70–73.
ne geswiceð: cf. Beowulf, v. 1460:
Næfre hit æt hilde ne swac
Manna ængum þara þe hit mid mundum gewand.
A 3. *Mimming*: Weland's most famous sword.
In þiðrik's saga, co. 57 ff., Mimir is Velent's master, Mimungr his
masterpiece; cf. Biterolf and Dietlieb, vv. 115–181, Horn Child, III. 298:
" It is the make of Miming,
Of all swerdes it is king,
And Weland it wrought,"

WALDHERE

A.

Eagerly she (sc. Hildegyth) encouraged him: "Weland's handiwork in very truth will fail no man who can wield the sharp Mimming. Many a time has warrior after warrior fallen in the fray, pierced by the sword and weltering in his blood. And in this hour, champion of Attila, let not thy prowess yield, thy knightly courage fail. Now is the day come when thou, son of Aelfhere, must lose thy life, or else win lasting glory among men. Never will I taunt thee with reproachful words, O lover mine, that in the clash of swords I have seen thee yield in craven fashion to the onset of any man, nor flee to the wall to save thy life, though many a foeman smote thy corselet with his sword. But ever didst thou strive to

and continental references. (Maurus, *Die Wielandsage*, passim.) In Saxo, Bk III., however, Mimingus is the name of the *satyrus* robbed by Hotherus of a sword and ring.

A 4. *hearne*, phonetic spelling of *heardne*, "sharp"; cf. Beowulf, v. 2067, *Heaðobearna*.

A 6. *Ætlan ordwyga*; cf. Waltharius, v. 106:
> *Militiae primos tunc Attila fecerat illos*;

Nibelungenlied, str. 1735:
> *Er und der von Spâne   trâten manegen stíc,*
> *Do si hie bi Etzel   vâhten manegen wîc.*

For Teutonic princes in the service of Attila, cf. Jordanes, c. XXXVIII.

A 7. *dryhtscipe*: *feallan* supplied by Stephens to complete the verse. This leaves a lacuna of half a verse at the beginning of the next line. Accordingly Holthausen would expunge *to dæge* and read:
> *ne læt ðin ellen nu gyt,*
> *gedreosan dryhtscipe.   Nu is se dæg cumen.*

A 8. [*Nu*] *is se dæg cumen.*
At the end of l. 7 of the MS. there is something illegible that may possibly be *nu* (Holthausen, *Die altenglischen Waldere-Bruchstücke*, p. 5); cf. Beowulf, v. 2646: *Nu is se dæg cumen.*

A 9. *oðer twega*; cf. Maldon, v. 207:
> *hie woldon þa ealle   oðer twega,*
> *lif forleosan   oððe leofne gewrecan.*

A 12—20, according to Heinzel (*Walthersage*, p. 7 ff.), refer to exploits in the service of Attila, which Hildegyth might possibly have witnessed from a tower or walled city; but the use of the demonstrative *ðam* most probably limits them to the preceding day, especially as Bugge compares with *weal* Waltharius, v. 1118:
> *Donec jam castrum securus deserat artum.*

gesawe: Cosijn explains it as poetic licence, "saw" for "heard."

Ac ðu symle furðor   feohtan sohtest
mæl ofer mearce.   Ðy ic ðe metod ondred
20 þæt ðu to fyrenlice   feohtan sohtest
æt ðam ætstealle   oðres monnes
wigrædenne.   Weorða ðe selfne
godum dædum,   ðenden ðin God recce.
Ne murn ðu for ði mece;   ðe wearð maðma cyst
25 gifeðe to eoce unc;   ðy ðu Guðhere scealt
beot forbigan,   ðæs ðe he ðas beaduwe ongan
mid unryhte   ærest secan.
Forsoc he ðam swurde   *ond* ðam syncfatum,
beaga mænigo;   nu sceal beaga leas
30 hworfan from ðisse hilde,   hlafurd secan
ealdne *eðel,*   oððe her ær swefan,
gif he ða......."

B.

"......[*me*]ce bæteran
buton ðam anum   ðe ic eac hafa
on stanfate   stille gehided.

A 25. MS. *gifede.*   31. MS. Ȝ.
B 1. MS. *ce.*

A 18.   *ac ðu symle furðor   feohtan sohtest,*
               mæl ofer mearce.
With the expression *sohtest mæl*, cf. the Icelandic legal term, *sœkja mál*,
"to press a suit." *Feohtan* is a noun in apposition to *mæl* and *ofer
mearce* = "into the enemy's country." The whole phrase may be translated "but ever thou didst seek to press home thy martial suit."
    A 19. *metod,* here, as originally, "fate," "destiny" (cf. O.N. *mjǫtuðr*);
usually an epithet applied to the Creator.
    A 20. *feohtan,* as in v. 18, to be taken as the acc. of *feohte* rather than
as a verb. The instances of *secan* + infinitive noted by Callaway (*The
Infinitive in Anglo-Saxon,* pp. 57, 286) are all taken from rather late prose
works.
    A 21. *æt ðam ætstealle:* *ætsteall* occurs twice elsewhere, in Guthlac,
v. 150:

        him to ætstælle   ærest arærde
        Cristes rode;   þær se cempa oferwon
        frecnessa fela;

and as a place-name *æt ætstealles beorh* in a charter of Cnut; cf. Kemble,
Codex Diplomaticus, IV. 31². The only translation which will suit all three
passages appears to be "position" in the military sense; cf. Waltharius,
v. 1103: *tali castro nec non statione locatus.*

press home thy martial suit. Wherefore I trembled for thy fate, for that too fiercely thou didst attack thy warlike adversary on the field of battle. Win honour for thyself by noble deeds and till then may God protect thee. Have no care for that sword; a peerless treasure is vouchsafed to thee to help us in our time of trouble; wherewith thou shalt humble Guthhere's pride, in that he unjustly began the strife against thee. He refused the sword and the casket of treasure with its many rings. Now ringless he shall leave this combat and return to the land of which he has long been lord, or perish here, if he...."

B.

" ......a better [sword] save that one which I too have laid at rest in its jewelled sheath. I know that Theodric

A **25**. *eoce*, phonetic for *geoce*; cf. Andreas, v. 1124, *eogoþe*, etc.

A **29**. In support of the emendation *bega leas*, "without either," which is not absolutely necessary, Bugge brings up Lokasenna, xiii.:

"*Jós ok armbauga   mundu æ vesa*
beggja vanr, Bragi."

A **30** ff., cf. Beowulf, v. 520 ff. (Cosijn).

B **1**. The interpretation of this passage is very doubtful. The fragment opens towards the end of a speech by Guthhere, just before the swords are drawn for the last struggle. Presumably Guthhere, who prides himself on the excellence of his equipment (cf. Atlakviþa, vii.:

Sjau eigum salhús   sverþa full hverju,
[hver eru þeira   hjǫlt ór golli].
Minn veitk mar baztan   mæki hvassastan),

declares that Waldhere possesses no sword better than his own.

The meaning of *stanfæt* is disputed; elsewhere it is used for a receptacle of stone, such as the alabaster pot of ointment, and a parallel to the whole passage occurs in the Metra of Boethius xx. 151:

ond on stanum eac   stille geheded.

The translation would then be "a better sword than that one which I have as well as this, stowed away in a stone-chest."

But would Guthhere have left his most precious sword at home on an occasion like this? Moreover *vaz* is used for "sheath" in MHG. and scabbards set with precious stones are occasionally found in continental graves of the migration period; cf. the sword-sheath set with garnets from the grave of Childeric (ob. 481), and the gold band with red stones from the grave of Pouan (of Theodoric the Visigoth, who fell in the battle of the Catalaunian Plains? Cf. Lindenschmit, *Handbuch der deutschen Alterthumskunde* i. 68, 232 ff.).

In this case it would be translated as above. For the use of *hydan* in this sense cf. *Homilies of Ælfric* (ed. Thorpe), ii. 246, 24,

Crist het hine hydan ðæt heard isern.

Bugge restores the verse as follows:

[Ne seah ic mid mannum   me]ce bæteran.

Ic wat þæt *hine* ðohte   Ðeodric Widian
5 selfu*m* onsendan   *ond* eac sinc micel
maðma mid ði mece,   monig oðres mid him
golde gegirwan—   iulean genam,
þæs ðe hine of nearwum   Niðhades mæg,
Welandes bearn,   Widia ut forlet—
10 ðurh fifela geweald   forð onette."
     Waldere maðelode,   wiga ellenrof, —
hæfde him on handa   hildefro[*f*]re
guðbilla gripe—   gyddode wordu*m* :
"Hwæt ðu huru wendest,   wine Burgenda,
15 þæt me Hagenan hand   hilde gefremede
ond getwænide feðewigges?   Feta, gif ðu dyrre,
æt ðus heaðuwerigan   hare byrnan.
Stanðed me her on eaxelu*m*   Ælfheres laf,
god *ond* geapneb,   golde geweorðod,
20 ealles unscende   æðelinges reaf
to habbanne,   þon*ne* ha[*n*]d wereð
feorhhord feondum;   *ne* bið fah wið me
þonne unmægas   eft ongynnað,
mecum gemetað,   swa ge me dydon.

B 4. MS. *ic.*   10. MS. *gefeald.*   12. MS. *hildefrore.*
18. MS. *standað.*   21. MS. *had.*   22. MS. *he.*

B **4**. Nonsense as it stands in the ms. Trautmann emends *ic* to *hine*
(the sword Mimming).
B **7—10**; cf. Witige's speech to Heime in Alpharts Tod, str. 252 ff.:
     Dar an solt dú gedenken,   dú uz ervelter degen
     wie ich dir kam ze helfe   unde vriste dir dín leben.
     Daz tet ich zuo Mûtâren,   dâ half ich dir uz nôt,
     dâ müestestû zewâre   den grimmelichen tôt
     dú und der von Berne   beide genomen hân
     wan daz ich in beiden   sô schiere ze helfe kam.
The whole question of Dietrich's captivity among the giants is treated by
Jiriczek, *Deutsche Heldensagen* i. 182–271. The following are the most
important passages in MHG. poetry:
     1. *Virginal* (Zupitza, *Deutsches Heldenbuch*, v. 1 ff.). Dietrich loses his
way near Castle Mutar, where Duke Nitger lives guarded by twelve giants.
He is captured by one of these giants and held in close confinement till he
wins the favour of Nitger's sister, who lets Hildebrand know of his master's
plight. Hildebrand, Witige, Heime and others hasten to his aid; the giants
are slain, the castle taken and Dietrich rescued from captivity.
     2. *Sigenot* (Zupitza, *D.H.B.* v. 207 ff.). Dietrich is again captured by
a giant and rescued by Hildebrand.
     3. *Laurin* (Jänicke, *D.H.B.* i. 199 ff.) treats of a captivity of Dietrich
among the dwarfs.
     A convenient summary of these poems will be found in F. E. Sandbach's
Heroic Saga-Cycle of Dietrich of Bern (London, 1905).

was minded to send it to Widia himself and much costly treasure with that blade and much beside it deck with gold. Nithhad's kinsman, Widia, the son of Weland, received the reward that had long been due for rescuing him from captivity. Through the giants' domain Theodric hastened forth."

Then spake Waldhere,—in his hand he grasped his trenchant blade, a comfort in the fray—the daring warrior, with defiant words : "Ha, friend of the Burgundians, didst thou deem in very truth that Hagena's hand had done battle with me and brought my days of combat to a close? Fetch, if thou darest, the grey corselet from me who am exhausted by the fray. Here it lies on my shoulders, even the heirloom of Aelfhere, good and broad-bossed and decked with gold, in every wise a glorious garment for a prince to wear, whose hand protects the treasure of his life against his foes. Never will it play me false, when faithless kinsmen return to the attack and beset me with their swords as ye have done.

B **10.** *gefeald*, which does not occur elsewhere, should be emended to *geweald*; cf. Beowulf, v. 903, *on feonda geweald* (Kluge).

B **12.** MS. *hildefrore* emended by Dietrich to *hildefrofre*. Cosijn points out that *frore* for *frofre* is also found in *The Rule of St Benet*, p. 10¹ (ed. Logeman, *E.E.T.S.* 1888).

B **13.** *guðbilla gripe*, abstract for concrete, "snijdend (tot den houw gereed) zwaard" [Cosijn], rather than "a gem of war-swords" (*gripe* = ON. *gripr*).

B **14.** *wine Burgenda*; cf. Atlakviþa, xix., *vin Borgunda* (emended to *Borgunda hollvin* by Gering), see introduction, p. 41.

B **19.** *geapneb* has been translated "well-arched" and "crooked-nibbed" (B.T.), neither of which epithets is particularly appropriate to a corselet. On the other hand a mail-coat, found by Engelhardt (*Denmark in the early Iron Age*, p. 46, etc.) in the peat-mosses of Torsbjærg and often figured since, was strengthened or decorated with breast-plates (*phalerae*); cf. the "zierschieben" of bronze in the museums of Kiel, Stettin, Hanover, etc., mentioned by Lindenschmit, *Die Alterthümer unserer heidnischen Vorzeit*, iii. vij. taf. 3. These *phalerae* were ultimately of Roman origin; cf. Daremberg-Saglio, *Dictionnaire des Antiquités grecques et romaines*, iv. 425, for examples from Crefeld and Mainz, especially the gravestone of M'. Caelius who fell with Varus, in 9 A.D. Is it impossible therefore that, as a shield with its boss is styled *cellod bord*, "the beaked shield," in Maldon, v. 283, so the epithet *geapneb*, "broad-bossed," should be applied to a mail-coat of this kind ?

B **23.** MS. *þon | un mægas* with a lacuna of three or four letters at the end of the line, which Stephens filled by the insertion of *yfle*. Bugge (*Tidskrift*, viii. 306) and Holthausen (*Beowulf* (3), ii. 173) declare that they can read *þon oʒ | un mægas*, though *ʒ* is found only in ON. MSS., not elsewhere in AS. *Onga*, the word they postulate, does occur in the sense of "sting," "point of an arrow" (Riddle xxiv. 4). They connect it with the

25 Ðeah mæg sige syllan   se ðe symle byð
   recon *ond* rædfest   ryhta gehwilces,
   se ðe him to ðam halgan   helpan gelifeð,
   to Gode gioce,   he þær gearo findeð,
   gif ða earnunga   ær geðenceð.
30 Þonne moten wlance   welan britnian
   æhtum wealdan,   þæt is...."

B 30.   MS. mtoten.

Frankish ἄγγων of Agathias, ɪɪ. 5, and graves of the Merovingian period; cf. too the *tridens* of Waltharius, v. 983 ff. (Althof, *W.P.* ɪɪ. 382). In this case *mægas* = *mæcgas,* "warriors" (Diether, *Anglia,* xɪ. 106).

It were better perhaps to keep the reading *þonne unmægas,* which, if demanding a ἅπαξ λεγόμενον, does fit in with sense and metre. *Unmægas*

Yet victory can be given by Him who is always prompt and regardful of everything that is good. For whosoever trusts in the Holy One for help, in God for succour, finds it ready to his hand, if first he be determined to deserve it. Thus can the great distribute their wealth and rule their possessions: that is......"

may be compared with such forms as *unlonde* (Walfisc, v. 14), "land that is no land," and translated "kinsmen who are no kinsmen."

B **26.** *recon;* unless the text be normalised, it is quite unnecessary to emend to *recen,* there being sufficient evidence for *recon* (B.T.).

FINN

......[*hor*]nas byrnað næfre.
Hleoþrode þa   hearogeong cyning:
"Ne ðis ne dagað eastan,   ne her draca ne fleogeð,
ne her ðisse healle   hornas ne byrnað;
5, 6 ac her forþ berað.   Fugelas singað,
gylleð græghama,   guðwudu hlynneð,
scyld scefte oncwyð.   Nu scyneð þes mona
waðol under wolcnum,   nu arisað weadæda
10 ðe ðisne folces nið   fremman willað.
Ac onwacnigeaþ nu,   wigend mine,
habbað eowre *h*lencan,   hic̄geaþ on ellen,
windað on orde,   wesað on mode."

1. Hickes * *nas.*   3. H. *eastun.*
12. H. *habbað eowre landa, hie geaþ on ellen.*

1. The fragment opens in the middle of a word; Grein (*Beowulf*, p. 75) supplies [*beorhtre hor*]*nas.*

2. *hleoþrode þa,* a satisfactory half-verse of the E type, though Trautmann and others would reverse the order on the analogy of Andreas, vv. 537, 1360, etc.

hearogeong cyning. Following Grundtvig all modern editors emend to *heaþogeong*—quite unnecessarily to my mind. *Hearogeong* (for *heorugeong*) is a perfectly admissible form, with the same meaning, whatever that may be, as *heaþogeong,* which is likewise a ἅπαξ λεγόμενον; cf. *heordra* for *heardra* in v. 28.

cyning, probably the Hengest of v. 19. He is however styled *þeodnes ðegn* in Beowulf, v. 1085. This may be a loose or proleptic usage of *cyning;* cf. Abbo, *de Bello Parisiaco,* I. 38: *Solo rex verbo, sociis tamen imperitabat;* and Chadwick, *Studies on Anglo-Saxon Institutions,* pp. 301 ff. (Cambridge, 1905).

3, 4. Cf. Grottasǫngr. xix.:

Eld sék brinna   *fyr austan borg:*
vigspjǫll vaka,   *þat mun viti kallaþr;*
mun her koma   *hinig of bragþi*
ok brenna bǿ   *fyr buþlungi.*

For the portent of a fiery dragon, cf. Saxo, Bk vi. (Holder, p. 175), and the Chronicle 793 E, *wæron geseuwene fyrene dracan on þam lyfte fleogende* (before the coming of the Northmen).

5, 6. *ac her forþ berað.* Most editors have assumed a lacuna of at least two half-lines after *berað.* Hence Grein (*Beowulf,* p. 75) would supply

feorhgeniðlan

fyrdsearu fuslicu
and Bugge (*P.B.B.* xii. 23),

fyrdsearu rincas

flacre flanbogan.

FINN

......Then cried the king young in war, "It is not dawn
that glows in the east. There is no dragon flying here, nor
are the gables of this hall aflame. But here they are hurrying forth. The birds are singing, the grey-coat is howling,
the war-wood is clanging, shield echoing when smitten by
the shaft. Now shines the moon through rifts in the clouds;
now fearful deeds are afoot that will bring on a pitched battle
here. But wake ye now, my warriors, don your corselets,
think on your prowess, dash to the van, be of good courage."

Schilling, however (*M. L. N.* I. 116 ff.) points out that no subject is required
in A.S. where one is perfectly well understood; cf. Pogatscher, *Anglia*, XXIII.
261 ff. Moreover *beraðˀ* is to be taken as intransitive. "But here they (the
Frisians) are hurrying forth"; cf. Elene, v. 45:

beran ut þrǽce
rincas under roderum,

and Andreas, v. 1220; also the mod. Eng. use of "bear" in nautical
phrases.

6, 7. There are several ways of taking this passage:

(1) *fugelas* = "arrows," not elsewhere in A.S., *grǽghama* = "mail-
coat"; cf. Beowulf, v. 334, *grǽge syrcan*, Andreas, v. 129, *guðˀsearo gullon*,
"The arrows are whistling, the mail-coat is rattling."

(2) *fugelas* = "birds of carrion," harbingers of slaughter, as often in
A.S. poetry; *grǽghama* = "wolf"; cf. Exeter Gnomic Verses, 151, *wulf se
grǽga*, Brunanburh, v. 64, etc.

The latter rendering is more in character.

8. *þes*, idiomatic usage; cf. Exodus, v. 430, *þeos geomre lyft*, etc.
(Klaeber, *Archiv f. n. S.* cxv. 181).

9. *waðˀol*; cf. perhaps MHG. *wadel*, "wandering," "erratic"; see
Chambers, *Beowulf*, p. 159.

10. *folces niðˀ* in the sense of *folcgefeoht, folcgewinn.*

12. Hickes, *habbaðˀ eowre landa, hie geaþ on ellen*, emended to *habbaðˀ
eowre hlencan, hicgeaþ on ellen* on the analogy of Elene, v. 218: *habban
heora hlencan, hycgan on ellen*; cf. Bugge, *P.B.B.* XII. 23.

hicgeaþ on ellen; cf. Atlamál, XLVI., *hugþi á harþrǽþi* and the Homeric
μνήσασθε δὲ θούριδος ἀλκῆς (*Iliad*, VI. 112).

13. *windaðˀ on orde*; cf. Genesis, v. 417:

þæt he mid feðˀerhoman   fleogan meahte
windan on wolcne.

The initial letter of *windaðˀ* is slightly different in form from the
customary *w* of Hickes. Hence Rieger (*Z.f.d.A.* XLVIII. 9) and Klaeber
(*E. St.* XXXIX. 428) read *þindaðˀ* = *tumescere*, "show your temper"; the
alliteration would then fall on *orde, onmode.* But cf. v. 27, *wreccea* (H.
wrecten), where the identical form of *w* is found and initial *þ* is out of the
question. Moreover Hickes represents capital *þ* by *Ð*, even where the MSS.
have *þ*: cf. Metra of Boethius, IV. 11, 12 ff. in *Thesaurus*, I. 185 and Grein-
Wülker, III. 7 ff.

D. R. P.   5

14,15 Ða aras mænig goldhladen ðegn, gyrde hine his
    swurde;
    ða to dura eodon   drihtlice cempan,
    Sigeferð and Eaha   hyra sword getugon
    and æt oþrum durum   Ordlaf and Guþlaf
    and Hengest sylf   hwearf him on laste.
20 Ða gyt Garulf   Guðere styrode
    ðæt he swa freolic feorh   forman siþe
    to ðære healle durum   hyrsta ne bær*e*
    nu hyt niþa heard   anyman wolde.
    ac he frægn ofer eal[*le*]   undearninga,
25 deormod hæleþ,   hwa þa duru heolde.
    "Sigeferð is min nama (cweþ he), ic eom Secgena
    leod,
    wrecc*ea* wide cuð;   fæla ic wean*a* gebad,
    heordra hilda.   Ðe is gyt her witod
    swæþer ðu sylf to me   secean wylle."
30 Ða wæs on healle   wælslihta gehlyn;
    sceolde cel*lod* bor*d*   cenum on handa

    22. H. *baeran.*   24. H. *eal.*   27. H. *wrecten, weuna.*
    31. H. *sceolde Celaes borð genumon handa.*

14. Apparently there is a half-verse missing here and Sievers (*Z.f.d.Ph.*
xxix. 563 ff.), regarding *goldhladen þegn* as unmetrical, would emend to
goldhladen gumþegn; cf. be Monna Cræfte, v. 83. Hence Holthausen
(*Z.f.d.Ph.* xxxvii. 123) proposes
      Ða aras [*of ræste*   *rumheort*] *mænig*
      goldhladen [*gum*]*þegn.*
But, as in Hildebrand, I prefer to print the MS. as prose.
    17. *Eaha*: this form with intervocalic *h* is declared impossible by
Möller (*ae. Volksepos*, p. 86), who would emend to *Eawa* (the name of
Penda's brother in Chronicle, 716 A, 757 A); but cf. *Echha* in Liber Vitae,
94, 96 (Sweet, *O.E.T.* p. 155 ff.), *Aehcha* in a charter of Wihtred, K. of
Kent (*O.E.T.* p. 428) and *Acha* (fem.) in Bede, *H.E.* iii. 6.
    18. *durum*, pl. for sing., as regularly in ON. *dyrr.*
    Ordlaf and Guþlaf; cf. the Oslaf and Guðlaf, who appear as Hnæf's
avengers in Beowulf, v. 1148 ff. The names Oddleivus and Gunnleivus are
also found in Arngrim Jónsson's epitome of the lost Skjöldunga saga, c. iv.;
cf. Chadwick, *O.E.N.* p. 52.
    19. *Hengest.* Chadwick (*O.E.N.* p. 52) has shown that there is some
reason for identifying this Hengest with the conqueror of Kent, the only
other person who bears the name.
    20 ff. It is just possible that Hickes' reading (with the emendation of
he to *he*[*o*]) may be taken.
    " Meanwhile Garulf (a Frisian) was taunting the warlike band (Hengest's
men), saying that such noble souls as they should not bear their armour to
the hall-door at the first onset, now that a bold warrior (Garulf himself) was
bent on spoliation."   [But

Then up rose many a knight bedecked with gold and buckled his sword about him. The lordly champions strode to the door; Sigeferth and Eaha drew their swords, and to the other door went Ordlaf and Guthlaf, and Hengest himself followed in their wake.

Meanwhile Guthhere was urging Garulf that he, whose life was so precious, should not bear his armour to the door of the hall at the first onset now that a fierce warrior was bent on spoliation. But he like a gallant hero demanded loudly above all the din of battle who it was that held the door. "Sigeferth is my name," said he. "I am prince of the Secgan, known as a rover far and wide. Many a hardship, many a fierce battle have I endured. Yet to thee is either lot assured that thou wilt seek at my hands."

Then there was the crash of deadly blows within the hall; the beaked shield in the heroes' hand must needs

But for my own part I am inclined to favour a more radical purge on the lines of Klaeber (*E. St.* xxxix. 307, adopted by Chambers):

þa gyt Garulfe Guðere styrde, etc.

"Meanwhile Guthhere was restraining Garulf (his nephew; cf. Hagano and Patavrid in Waltharius, v. 846; Hildebrand and Wolfhart in Nibelungenlied, str. 2208 ff.), saying that he, whose life was so precious, should not bear his armour to the hall-door at the first onset, now that so bold a warrior (Sigeferth) was bent on spoliation; but he (Garulf)...."

23. *hyt*, loose usage for *hie* (*hyrsta*); cf. Beowulf, v. 1705 (Klaeber, *Anglia*, xxviii. 456).

24. Hickes, *eal*. Trautmann (*B.B.* vii. 44) emends to *ealle* on metrical grounds; cf. Beowulf, v. 2899: *sægde ofer ealle*, and Daniel, v. 528:

frægn ofer ealle
Swiðmod cyning   hwæt þæt swefen bode.

26. *Sigeferþ, Secgena leod*, doubtless the *Sæferð* who ruled the *Sycgan* in Widsith, v. 31. For the confusion of *Sæ*- and *Sige*-, cf. Sæberht, K. of the East Saxons, who appears as *Saberchtus* or *Saeberchtus* in the text of Bede, but as *Sigberchtus* in certain mss. of the *Chronological Summary* (Plummer, *Baedae Opera Historica* ii. 353); cf. Chambers, *Widsith*, p. 199.

Uhland (*Germ.* ii. 357 ff.) and Golther (*Germ.* xxxiii. 474–5) identify this *Sigeferþ* with Sigurd the Vǫlsung, but their views have met with little support.

⟨cweþ he⟩: the only instance in AS. of the parenthetical "said he," so common in Hildebrand and the Heliand.

30. Cf. Saxo, Bk ii. (Holder, p. 65):

Iam curia bellis
Concutitur diroque strepunt certamine portae.

31, perhaps the greatest crux in AS. poetry. Hickes is quite unintelligible; Grein (*Beowulf*, p. 76) emends to

sceolde cellod bord   cenum on handa,
banhelm berstan,

comparing Maldon, v. 283, *clufon cellod bord*, where *cellod* probably means "beaked" (Bosworth-Toller; cf. Epinal Gloss. 862: *rostrum=neb vel scipes celae*), no unsuitable epithet for an Anglo-Saxon shield. There are many

banhelm berstan;   buruhðelu dynede,
oð æt ðære guðe   Garulf gecrang
ealra ærest   eorðbuendra,
35 Guðlafes sunu;   ymbe hyne godra fæla,
†hwearflacra hraer.†   Hræfen wandrode
sweart and sealobrun,   swurdleoma stod,
swylce eal Finn[e]sburuh   fyrenu wære.
Ne gefrægn ic næfre wurþlicor   æt wera hilde
40 sixtig sigebeorna   sel gebærann,
ne næfre swanas hwitne medo   sel forgyldan,
ðonne Hnæfe guldan   his hægstealdas.
Hig fuhton fif dagas,   swa hyra nan ne feol
drihtgesiða,   ac hig ða duru heoldon.
45   Ða gewat him wund hæleð   on wæg gangan,
sæde þæt his byrne   abrocen wære,
heresceorpum hror,   and eac wæs his helm ðyrl.
Ða hine sona frægn   folces hyrde
hu ða wigend   hyra wunda genæson,
50 oððe hwæþer ðæra hyssa.......

38. H. *Finnsburuh.*   41. H. *swa noc.*   44. H. *dura.*

other suggestions [Trautmann, *B.B.* vii. 46, *cyllod*, "covered with leather," from *cyll*, "a leather pouch"; Jellinek, *P.B.B.* xv. 431, *celed*; cf. Beowulf, v. 3022, *gar morgenceald*; Holthausen *ceorlæs* (collect. sg.), later *clæne*, etc.]; but Grein still holds the field.

banhelm may be taken as a kenning for shield, either:
(1) *bănhelm*=munimentum adversus occisores (*Sprachschatz*) or
(2) *bănhelm*=*bānhus-helm*, "protection for the frame," though in similar compounds *ban*=ON. *bein*; e.g. *banbeorgas, banryft*=*ocreae*. In either case *berstan* would be intransitive.
"The beaked shield...must needs be shattered."
Bugge, however (*P.B.B.* xii. 26) would emend to *bar-helm*, "boar-helmet," and take *berstan* as transitive, so in Riddle v. 8, and often in Middle English.
"The beaked shield...must needs shatter the boar-helmet";
cf. Tacitus, *Agricola*, c. xxxvi.: *Igitur et Batavi miscere ictus, ferire umbonibus, ora foedare*; and Waltharius, v. 195:
Sternitur et quaedam pars duro umbone virorum.
Unfortunately *bār* does not occur in Anglo-Saxon poetry. But cannot *bănhelm* be retained in the sense of "helmet decorated with bones" (horns); cf. the epithets applied to Heorot in Beowulf, v. 704, *hornreced*, v. 780, *banfah*? This view is quite unobjectionable on philological grounds and is supported by archaeological evidence. Of course there are no such helmets in existence from the Germanic area. Helmets of any description are comparatively rare and, decorated with horns, are found only in representation; e.g. alongside boar-helmets on the bronze plates from Torslunda, Öland (Stjerna, *Essays on Beowulf*, p. 8); on the silver disc from Neuwied (Althof, *WalthArii Poesis*, ii. 398); on the Golden Horn of Gallehus and the Gundestrup bowl (Müller, *Nordische Altertumskunde*, ii. 155, 165). For

shatter the horned helm.   The castle floor reechoed, till in
the fray fell Garulf, son of Guthlaf, first of dwellers upon
earth, and many a gallant warrior about him ;....... The
raven hovered dismal with its dusky plumage; the gleam of
swords flashed forth as though all Finn's castle were aflame.

Never have I heard of sixty warriors flushed with victory
who bore themselves more gallantly nor more honourably
in mortal conflict, nor squires who paid a better recompense
for shining mead than did his retinue to Hnaef.   Five days
they fought in such a wise that no man fell out of that
knightly band; but still they held the door.

Then departed a wounded hero limping from the fray;
he said that his mailcoat, armour of proof, was shattered and
pierced likewise was his helm.   Him straightway asked the
keeper of the host how those warriors survived their wounds,
or which of the heroes......

non-Germanic, Mycenaean, Macedonian, Celtic, instances, cf. Daremberg-
Saglio, II. 1438 ff., s.v. *galea*.
36. Hickes' *hwearflacra hraer* is corrupt, and none of the many
emendations (Grundtvig, *hwearflicra hræw* ; Bugge, *P.B.B.* XII. 27 : *hwearf*
[*f*]*lacra hræw*) are at all convincing.   Those editors who see a verb in *hraer*
are perhaps nearer the mark (Jellinek, *P.B.B.* XV. 431, *hwearf laðra
hreas*) ; and Holthausen's *hwearf* [*b*]*lacra hreas*, "a company of pale ones
fell," is supported by Beowulf, v. 2488, *hreas* [*hilde*]*blac*.
38. Hickes, *Finnsburuh*, an impossible form in AS.
41. Grein (*Beowulf*, p. 76) emends Hickes to *ne næfre swanas swetne
medo sel forgyldan*. *Swanas* is obviously correct; but since the metre is
corrupt again, there is no point in altering *hwitne*.
44. *duru*: probably Hickes misread *u* for *a* in the MS., as in v. 3 *eastun*,
v. 27 *weuna*.
47. *heresceorpum hror*. Thorpe emends to *heresceorp unhror*, "his
armour useless," though it is doubtful whether *unhror* can bear this
meaning; cf. however, Chambers, *Beowulf*, p. 162. But the MS. reading
can be translated "strong as armour" (Bosworth-Toller).
48. *folces hyrde*: Finn; cf. the common Homeric expression ποιμένα
λαῶν, "shepherd of the host," applied especially to Agamemnon.

DEOR

Weland †himbe wurman†   wræces cunnade,
anhydig eorl   earfoþa dreag,
hæfde him to gesiþþe   sorge ond longaþ,
wintercealde wræce;   wean oft onfond,

1. *Weland*, the most celebrated smith of old Teutonic legend, mentioned over and over again in the literature of the middle ages. The references, English, German, Scandinavian and French, are collected by Maurus, *Die Wielandsage*, pp. 7–57 (*Münchener Beiträge*, xxv., Erlangen, 1902); cf. especially King Alfred's Translation of the Metra of Boethius, x. 33:

> *Hwær sint nu þæs wisan   Welandes ban*
> *þæs goldsmiðes,   þe wæs geo mærost;*

and Þiðriks saga, c. 69 (Bertelsen, II. 105):

> *Velent er sva frægr um alla norðrhalfo heimsins at sva þyckiaz allir menn mega mest lofa hans hagleic er hveria þa smið er betr er gor en annat smiði, at sa er Volundr at hagleic er gort hevir.*

Hence any weapon of especial excellence was ascribed to Weland; cf. Beowulf, v. 455, *Welandes geweorc* (of B.'s corselet); Waldhere, A 2 (of the sword Mimming); Waltharius, v. 965, *Wielandia fabrica* (of a mailcoat), etc.

The story mentioned here is found at length in the Old Norse *Vǫlundarkviþa*, one of the earliest of the Edda poems.

Briefly summarised, the story runs as follows: Vǫlundr, a mysterious smith, is surprised by Niþoþr, king of the Niarar, and robbed of a great treasure, including a (magic?) ring. The ring is given by Niþoþr to his daughter Boþvildr and the smith hamstrung to prevent reprisals. Forced to labour for the king, he seeks an opportunity for revenge, which soon presents itself. Visited in secret by Niþoþr's sons, he slays them both and makes of their bones utensils for the royal table. In the meantime Boþvildr has broken her ring and, fearing her father's wrath, she brings it to the smithy for repair. The smith receives her amiably and offers her wine to drink; but the draught is drugged and Vǫlundr works his will upon the sleeping princess. Once more in possession of the ring, he regains his magic power and flies away, first announcing what has happened to the king.

An expanded version of the Vǫlundr story, owing something to German influence, is found in Þiðriks saga, c. 57 ff. (Bertelsen, I. 73 ff.). There Velent is affiliated to the giant Vaði, the Wada of Widsith, whereas in Vǫlundarkviþa itself he is called *visi álfa*, "prince of the elves," in the prose introduction "son of the king of the Finns." Moreover the son of Boþvildr and Vǫlundr, vaguely hinted at in Vǫlundarkviþa, plays an important part in Þiðriks saga. He is Viðga, the Widia-Wudga of Widsith,

DEOR

Weland, the steadfast warrior, had experience of persecution; he suffered hardship. As boon companions he had
grief and yearning, misery in the cold of winter. He fell on

v. 130, and Waldhere, B 4, the famous Wittich of the MHG. Dietrich cycle.
This person seems to be identical with the Gothic hero Vidigoia of Jordanes,
cc. v. and xxxiv. Possibly there was something mysterious about the
parentage of this Vidigoia; he may have been the offspring of a Gothic
princess and a bondsmith [Chadwick, *H.A.* p. 135], and since smiths were
generally regarded as uncanny people, a folk-tale—cf. the Gascon *Pieds d'Or*,
edited by Bladé, *Contes Populaires de Gascogne*, I. 126-147 (Paris, 1886)—
may have been superimposed upon the original heroic story.

The second and third words are quite unintelligible; they are usually
printed *him be wurman*, and a host of suggestions, probable and improbable,
are collected in Grein-Wülker, I. 278 n. *Wurman* might conceivably be a
blundered place or tribal name. Tupper for instance (*Mod. Phil.* IX. 266)
suggests that we should keep the MS. reading and translate "in Werma-
land" (the S. Swedish district of Värmland, which is associated in the
Heimskringla, Olafs saga Helga, cc. 77, 181, with the neighbouring Nerike
and West Götaland; see v. 14 n.).

4. *wintercealde*; twice elsewhere in AS., Andreas, v. 1265, and Ridd.
v. 7, where it seems to mean "in the cold of winter"; cf. þiðriks saga, c. 73
(ed. Bertelsen, I. 117):

*Velent mælir at þeir skulo ganga ofgir til smiðionnar þegar snior væri
nyfallin. En sveinarnir hirða aldregi hvart þeir ganga ofgir eða rettir, en
þetta hefir um vetrinn veret. Oc þa samo nott eptir fell snior.*

In English tradition Weland is connected with a famous cromlech known
as Wayland Smith near Ashdown in Berkshire; cf. a letter from Francis
Wise to Dr Mead, printed in Warton's *History of English Poetry from the
Twelfth to the Close of the Sixteenth Century* (ed. by W. C. Hazlitt, London,
1871), I. 63 ff. :

"All the account which the country people are able to give of it is :
at this place lived formerly an invisible Smith, and if a traveller's horse had
left a shoe upon the road, he had no more to do than to bring the horse to
this place with a piece of money, and leaving both there for some little time
he might come again and find the money gone but the horse new shoed."

A similar story, told of the volcanic isle of Strongyle, is found in the
Scholia to Apollonius Rhodius, *Argonautica*, II. 761, and silent barter of
this kind still existed among the Veddahs of Ceylon in the days of Knox
(1681); cf. Seligman, *The Veddahs*, p. 6 ff. (Cambridge, 1911).

For the smith in tradition, see Schrader, *Sprachvergleichung u. Urge-
schichte₃*, II. 13-28 (Jena, 1907), and for the Weland story generally
Jiriczek, *Deutsche Heldensagen*, pp. 1-54 (Strassburg, 1898), and Clarke,
Sidelights on Teutonic History, pp. 201-8 (Cambridge, 1911).

5 siþþan hine Niðhad on   nede legde,
  swoncre seonobende   on syllan monn.
  þæs ofereode;   þisses swa mæg.

  Beadohilde ne wæs   hyre broþra deaþ
  on sefan swa sar   swa hyre sylfre þing,
10 þæt heo gearolice   ongieten hæfde
  þæt heo eacen wæs;   æfre ne meahte
  þriste geþencan,   hu ymb þæt sceolde.
  þæs ofereode;   þisses swa mæg.

  We þæt Mæðhilde   monge gefrugnon
15 wurdon grundlease   Geates frige,

14. MS. *mæð hilde.*

5. *on* should be included in the first half-line. An exactly parallel expression is found in Christ and Satan, v. 539:

  þec gelegdon on   laðne bend
  hæðene mid hondum.

6. *seonobende*; for the use of sinews as ropes, cf. Judges xvi. 7, *mid rapum of sinum geworhte* (A.V. "with seven green withs that were never dried").

For the whole passage, cf. Vǫlundarkviþa, xiv.:

  Vissi ser á hǫndum   hǫfgar nauþir
  En á fótum   fjǫtur of spentan.

Vǫlundr kvaþ:

  "*Hverir 'u jǫfrar   þeirs á lǫgþu*
  bestisima   ok mik bundu."

Several editors (see Grein-Wülker, I. 278 n.) have wished to read into the stanza the story of the maiming of Vǫlundr; cf. the prose between strophes XVIII. and XIX. of Vkv.: *Svá var gǫrt at skornar váru sínar í knesfótum ok settr í holm einu.*

They therefore emend *seonobende* to *seonobenne*, "wound to sinew," and translate "after Nithhad had laid him in bonds (and laid) a supple sinew-wound on a better man." But such emendation is quite unnecessary.

7. *ofereode*, impersonal with gen. of respect; cf. Shipley, *The Genitive case in Anglo-Saxon Poetry* (Baltimore, 1903), pp. 18, 50: Brandl's rendering (*P. G.*₂ II. 975), "das ging vorüber, dieses (gehe vorüber) wie es kann," seems unnecessarily strained.

8. *Beadohilde*, the daughter of Niðhad; her brothers had been slain and she herself outraged by Weland, as can be seen from the ON. Vǫlundarkviþa and þiðriks saga, c. 78, especially Vǫlundarkviþa XXXVIII.: *Nu gengr Bǫþvildr barni aukin.* Elsewhere her name occurs only as the Buodell of the Danish ballad, Kong Diderik og hans Kæmper, B 15 (Grundtvig, *Danmarks Gamle Folkeviser*, I. 100, Kjøbenhavn, 1853):

  Werlandt heder min fader,
  war en smedt well skǿn:
  Buodell hede min moder,
  en koning-dather wen.

The son of Beadohild and Weland was the Widia (Wudga) of Widsith, v. 124–130, and Waldhere B, v. 4–10, the Viðga of þiðriks saga, and the Wittich of the Dietrich cycle in MHG. literature. He was undoubtedly the Vidigoia, "the bravest of the Goths, who fell by the treachery of the Sarmatians," and was celebrated by his people in heroic poetry; cf. Jordanes, *de Origine Actibusque Getarum*, cc. v., XXXIV.

evil days after Nithhad had laid fetters upon him, supple
bonds of sinew on a nobler man.

That was surmounted; so can this be.

On Beadohild's mind her brothers' death preyed far less
sorely than her own condition, when she clearly perceived
that she was with child; she could not bear to think on
what must happen.

That was surmounted; so can this be.

Many of us have heard that the Geat's affection for

---

14. MS. *we þæt mæð hilde monge gefrugnon.*

A number of editors retain this reading and connect *mæð* (elsewhere
unknown in AS.) with the ON. *meiða*, translating "Many of us have heard
of Hild's violation." They cannot agree, however, upon the identity of the
lady. Gummere (*O.E.E.* p. 185) suggests Odila, the wife of Sifka, outraged
by Erminrik in Þiðriks saga, c. 276 (Bertelsen, ii. 158 ff.). Perhaps the most
plausible of these explanations is that put forward by Frederick Tupper, Jr
(*Mod. Phil.* ix. 265 ff.); he suggests that this, like the preceding stanzas,
refers to the Weland story. The Geat he identifies with Niðhad (cf. Vkv. ix.,
Niþoþr Niara dróttin="lord of Nerike," a part of the Swedish Götaland
in medieval times), the Hild with Beadohild. With v. 16 he compares
Vkv. xxxiii. :

> Vaki ek ofvalt   viljalauss,
> sofna ek minst   síz sunu dauþa.

But elsewhere in AS. *frige* is used for sexual rather than parental love.
Besides the story of Niðhad and Widia, the son of Beadohild and Weland
(Niduda? and Vidigoia in Jordanes) is almost certainly of Gothic origin and
little likely to be connected with Sweden (as in Vkv.) in a poem so early as
Deor.

With less probability Lawrence (*Mod. Phil.* ix. 29 ff.) argues that it deals
with the love of Hild and Heðinn, comparing particularly the version found
in Saxo, Bk v.

But the case is far from proven, and it is safer to regard this stanza as
alluding to one of those stories, familiar enough to an Anglo-Saxon audience,
which have not come down to us. Klaeber (*Anglia*, Beiblatt, xvii. 283 ff.)
regards *mæð hilde* as the Dat. of a compound name, *Mæðhilde*. For the
use of Mæð- as the first element of a personal name there is at least one
parallel in the *Mæðhelm* of Liber Vitae, 96 (Sweet, *O.E.T.* p. 156). It is
perhaps derived by haplology from Mæðelhild, for the first element of which
cf. the Frankish Mallobaudes (Schönfeld, *Wörterbuch der Germanischen
Personen- und Volkernamen*, p. 159).

The name Geat does occur at the head of the West-Saxon and Bernician
genealogies, and in Old Norse literature there are a number of kings called
Gautr (Chadwick, *O.E.N.* p. 270); but there is nothing to connect this Geat
with them. It should be taken therefore as a national rather than a
personal name; Beowulf is spoken of as *Geat* in vv. 1715, 1792.

The Scandinavian story of the god Freyr's love for the giantess Gerðr
(found in Skírnismál, xliii.:

> Long es nótt,   langar 'u tvær,
> hvé of þreyjak þriar?
> Opt mér mónuþr   minni þótti
> an sjá hýngtt holf ;

and Gylfaginning, c. xxxvii. : *ekki svaf hann, ekki drakk hann; engi þorði
at krefja hann málsins*) is interesting as a parallel but nothing more.

þæt him seo sorglufu　　　slæp ealle binom.
þæs ofereode;　　　þisses swa mæg.

Ðeodric ahte　　　þritig wintra
Mæringa burg;　　　þæt wæs monigum cuþ.
20　　þæs ofereode;　　　þisses swa mæg.

We geascodon　　　Eormanrices
wylfenne geþoht;　　　ahte wide folc
Gotena rices;　　　þæt wæs grim cyning.
Sæt secg monig　　　sorgum gebunden,
25　　wean on wenan,　　　wyscte geneahhe
þæt þæs cynerices　　　ofercumen wære.
þæs ofereode;　　　þisses swa mæg.

16. MS. *hi.*

18. *Ðeodric.* With the notable exception of Wilhelm Grimm most authorities have identified Dietrich von Bern, the Theodoric of legend, with the historical king of the Ostrogoths, who conquered Italy from Odovacar and ruled it with great success from 493 to 527. It is certain that he was so identified in Anglo-Saxon literature; for the passages *þæt wæs Theodoricus se cyning þone we nemnaþ þeodric* in the *Old English Martyrology* (p. 84, ed. Herzfeld, *E.E.T.S.*) and *se þeodric wæs Amulinga* in *King Alfred's Old English Translation of Boethius* (p. 7, ed. Sedgefield, Oxford, 1899) equate the historical Theodoric with the hero of popular tradition. Yet there are certain striking differences; for the most notable features of the MHG. Dietrich story, found already in Hildebrand, are the thirty years of exile at the Hunnish court and the loss of almost all his knights—which find no counterpart in the life of the historical Theodoric. It seems most probable therefore that the Dietrich of tradition has been credited with adventures, which belong more properly to some older Gothic hero; perhaps his father, Theodemer, whose name indeed is found in the ms. of the Older Edda (e.g. *þjóþmár* of Guþrúnarkviþa, III. 3), perhaps the Gensimundus *toto orbe cantabilis* of Cassiodorus; cf. Chadwick, *Heroic Age*, p. 62.

19. *Mæringa burg.* A most striking parallel is to be found on the 10th century Runic stone from Rök in Östergötland, Sweden; cf. Bugge, *Antiqvarisk Tidskrift för Sverige*, v. 1 ff., and Stephens, *Handbook of the Old Northern Runic Monuments*, p. 32 ff. (London, 1884):

raiþ [þ]iaurikʀ　　　hin þurmuþi
stiliʀ flutna　　　[ą] strantu hraiþmaraʀ.
sitir nu karuʀ　　　ą kuta sinum
skialti ub fatlaþr　　　skati marika.

"Theodoric the bold was riding,
prince of warriors, on the shores of the Gothic sea [Adriatic].
He is sitting armed on his steed,
decked with a shield, the lord of the Mæringas."

This strophe is supposed to be a description of the equestrian statue of M. Aurelius, ascribed to Theodoric by the barbarians, which stood at Ravenna till removed by Charlemagne to Aachen in 809; cf. Torp, *Ark.f.n.F.* XXIX. 345 ff.

Mæringas, evidently a name applied to the Ostrogoths; elsewhere we find in the Regensburg Gloss *Gothi = Meranare*, and in the Latin prologue to Notker's OHG. translation of Boethius Theodoric is called *rex Mergothorum et Ostrogothorum.*

For the connection between Dietrich and the Tyrolese Meran in MHG.

Maethhild passed all bounds, that his hapless love completely robbed him of his sleep.

That was surmounted; so can this be.

Theodric ruled for thirty years the fortress of the Maeringas; that has become a matter of common knowledge.

That was surmounted; so can this be.

We have learned of Eormanric's ferocious disposition; he held dominion far and wide in the realm of the Goths. A cruel king was he. Many a man sat in the toils of care, anticipating trouble and continually praying for the downfall of his sovereignty.

That was surmounted; so can this be.

literature, cf. Heinzel, *Über die ostgotische Heldensage*, pp. 9 ff. (Wien, 1889); Jiriczek, *D.H.S.* i. 119 ff.

21. *Eormanrices.* According to his contemporary, Ammianus Marcellinus, xxxi. 3. 1, Ermenrichus was a great king of the Goths, his empire stretching from the Baltic to the Euxine, who perished by his own hand, despairing of resistance to the Huns, c. 375. After Theodoric he was the most celebrated in tradition of the Gothic kings; but he bears a most sinister character throughout. Widsith, v. 88 ff., credits him with generosity, but styles him *wraþ wærloga,* an epithet elsewhere applied to the Devil, and Beowulf, v. 1200, speaks of his *searoniðas* (murderous wiles); cf. too the Quedlinburg Annals: *astutior in dolo, largior in dono.* Already in the 6th century Jordanes, c. xxiv., relates that he was attacked and disabled by the kinsmen of Sunilda, whom he had torn asunder by wild horses, *pro mariti fraudulento discessu,* whatever that may mean.

There are three main elements in the later story of Eormanric (Jiriczek, *D.H.S.* i. 99). 1. The slaying of Swanhild and the vengeance taken by her brothers. 2. The death of his son. 3. The murder of the Harlungs (the Herelingas, Emerca and Fridla, of Widsith, v. 112); his persecution of Dietrich is peculiar to the German version.

From the 9th century at least the story developed on independent lines in Germany and Scandinavia. The Northern authorities, Bragi's Ragnarsdrápa, the Hamðismál, the Prose Edda and the Volsunga Saga (with the exception of Saxo, who only knows the Nibelung story from Low German sources; cf. Bk xiii., p. 427, *notissimam Grimilde erga fratres perfidiam*) connect it with their greatest hero Sigurd Fáfnisbani; Swanhild, daughter of Sigurd and Guðrun, is avenged by her brothers Hamðir and Sorli, Jormunrekk's hands and feet being cut off. In Germany, on the other hand, Eormanric is attracted into the Dietrich cycle; Dietrich is represented as his nephew, though we know from historical sources that he was born some eighty years after the former's death. In Middle High German literature (Dietrich's Flucht, etc.), as also in þiðriks saga, Eormanric is the wicked uncle of tradition; he compasses the death of his two nephews, the Harlungs, Dietrich the third he deprives of his kingdom. In the latter role he has evidently displaced Odovacar; cf. Hildebrand, v. 18.

For an exhaustive treatment of Eormanric in tradition, see Jiriczek, *D.H.S.* i. 55–118; Clarke, *Sidelights on Teutonic History*, pp. 232 ff.; Chambers, *Widsith*, pp. 15–36.

22. *wylfenne,* "wolfish," "ferocious"; cf. Heliand, v. 5059: *habdiun im hugi wulßo* (of the Jews).

Siteð sorgcearig,   sælum bedæled
on sefan sweorceð;   sylfum þinceð
30 þæt sy endeleas   earfoða dæl.

Mæg þonne geþencan,   þæt geond þas woruld
witig dryhten   wendeþ geneahhe,
eorle monegum   are gesceawað,
wislicne blæd,   sumum weana dæl.
35 þæt ic bi me sylfum   secgan wille,
þæt ic hwile wæs   Heodeninga scop,
dryhtne dyre;   me wæs Deor noma.
Ahte ic fela wintra   folgað tilne,
holdne hlaford,   oþ þæt Heorrenda nu,
40 leoðcræftig monn,   londryht geþah,
þæt me eorla hleo   ær gesealde.
þæs ofereode;   þisses swa mæg.

30. MS. *earfoda*.

31. Cf. Wanderer, v. 58:
    For þon ic geþencan ne mæg   geond þas woruld,
    for hwan modsefa   min ne gesweorce
    þonne ic eorla lif   eal geondþence;
a characteristic mood in Anglo-Saxon literature.

36. *Heodeninga scop*: *Heodeningas* = "Heoden and his men," cf. ON. *Hjaðningar* in the kenning *Hjaðninga veðr*: "battle" (Skaldsk. c. XLIX.), and MHG. *Hegelingas* (the form should be *Hetelingas*, but it has been influenced by certain Bavarian place-names; cf. Jiriczek, *Northern Hero-Legends*, p. 134) of the Austrian poem Kudrun.

Heðinn and Høgni—*Hagena weold Holmrygum, Heoden Glommum* of Widsith, v. 21—and the story of their everlasting conflict are known from all parts and all ages of the Scandinavian world, in the Ragnarsdrápa of Bragi Boddason, the earliest of Norwegian skalds, in the Háttalykill of Røgnvaldr, Jarl of the Orkneys (12th cent.), in the Icelandic Prose Edda of Snorri Sturlason, in the Sørlaþáttr, in the Faroese Sjurðar Kvæði—where, curiously enough, Høgni is confused with his namesake of the Nibelung story—and in a Shetland ballad of 1774 from the isle of Foula. The better-known of these versions are collected and translated by Chambers, *Widsith*, p. 100 ff. In Kudrun, however, Hetele and Hagen are reconciled; cf. Panzer, *Hilde-Gudrun*, passim (Halle, 1901).

He who is anxious and distressed sits bereft of joy, with
gloomy thoughts in his heart. Suffering, he deems, will
ever be his lot. Still he can reflect that the wise Lord
follows very different courses throughout the world; to many
a man he gives honour and abiding prosperity, yet nought
but misery to some.

Of myself I will say this much, that once I was minstrel
of the Heodeningas, my master's favourite. My name
was Deor. For many years I had a goodly office and
a generous lord, till now Heorrenda, a skilful bard, has
received the estate which the protector of warriors gave to
me in days gone by.

That was surmounted; so can this be.

37. *Deor.* The name Deor (in the form Diar) occurs in a Kentish
charter of 859; cf. Sweet, *O.E.T.* p. 450. It is also found on a coin of
Coenwulf of Mercia (796–822); and Aethelwulf of Wessex had a moneyer
of that name at Canterbury; cf. Grüber and Keary, *Catalogue of English
Coins in the B.M., Anglo-Saxon series*, I. 34, II. 9 ff. (London, 1887–93).

39. *Heorrenda*, like the Horant of Kudrun, is Heoden's minstrel. In
the Prose Edda (Skaldks. c. xlix.) and Sǫrlaþáttr, however, Hjarrandi is
become the father of Heðinn, though a tradition of the poet may have
survived in the Hjarrandaljóð mentioned in Bósa saga, c. xii. (*F.A.S.* III.
264).

40. *londryht*; as in Beowulf, v. 2886:

> *londrihtes mot*
> *þære mægburge   monna æghwylc*
> *idel hweorfan,*

seems to mean an "estate" (or the rights over one), granted by the king and
revocable at his pleasure; cf. Widsith, v. 95:

> *he me lond forgeaf*
> *mines fæderes eþel,   frea Myrginga.*

HILDEBRAND

Ik gihorta đat seggen
đat sih urhettun   ǽnon muotin,
Hildibra*n*t enti Hađubra*n*t,   untar heriun tuem.
Sunufatarungo   iro saro rihtun,
5 garutun se iro gu*đ*hamun,   gurtun sih iro suert ana,
helidos ubar [*h*]ringa;   do sie to dero hiltiu ritun.
Hiltibra*n*t gimahalta, (Heribrantes sunu,)   her uuas
    heroro man,
ferahes frotoro,   her fragen gistuont
fohem uuortum,   [*h*]wer sin fater wari
10,11 fireo in folche,   "eddo [*h*]welihhes cnuosles du sis?

.   .   .   .

ibu du mi ẹnan sages,   ik mi de odre uuet,
chind, in chunincriche: chud ist mi*r* al irmindeot."
Hadubrant gimahalta,   Hiltibrantes sunu :
15 "Đat sagetun mir   usere liuti,
alte anti frote,   dea érhina warun,

---

3. MS. *Hildibraht.*   6. MS. *ringa.*   7. MS. *Hiltibraht.*
9. MS. *wer.*   11. MS. *welihhes.*   13. MS. *min.*

1. *Ik gihorta đat seggen,* a regular epic formula in the old Teutonic languages.
2. *urhettun* might be N. pl. of a noun corresponding to AS. *oretta,* or the pret. pl. of a weak verb ; cf. Goth. *ushaitjan.*
ǽnon, probably N. pl. of adjective ; cf. Heliand, v. 13, *énon* (MS. *enan*).
muotin has been interpreted as the imperfect subj. of a verb corresponding to OS. *motian,* as the pret. pl. of *muoen,* "bemühen," "bedrängen" ; or as the G. sg. of a noun, for which however there appears to be no evidence in OHG. nor OS. But cf. Braune, *Ahd. Lesebuch,* pp. 180–1.
4. *Sunufatarungo,* a representative of a class of nouns—"dvandva compounds"—common in Sanskrit ; cf. OS. *gisunfader,* "father and sons" (Heliand, v. 1176) : AS. *suhtergefæderan,* "uncle and nephew" (Beowulf, v. 1164), etc. It might conceivably be an old dual ; otherwise it must be a G. pl. depending on *heriun.* Cf. Braune, p. 181.

HILDEBRAND

I have heard it said that Hildebrand and Hadubrand challenged each other to single combat between the hosts. Father and son, they set their panoply aright and made their armour ready: the heroes girt their swords above their corselets when they rode to the fray.

Hildebrand spake, the son of Heribrand: he was the older man, the riper in years. He began to ask in a few brief words who was his father among mortal men, "or of what stock art thou? If, young warrior, thou wilt tell me the name of one man in the kingdom, I shall know the others of myself; for the whole race of men is known to me."

Then spake Hadubrand, the son of Hildebrand: "Our liegemen, full of years and wisdom, who lived in days gone

7. *Heribrantes sunu* extra metrical as in vv. 30, 49, 58.
8. *ferahes frotoro*; cf. Maldon, v. 317: *ic eom frod feores.*
9. *fohem uuortum*; cf. Beowulf, v. 2246: *fea worda cwæð.*
     [*h*]*wer sin fater wari*
         fireo in folche;
v. Grienberger takes *fireo* with *hwer*; cf. *Odyssey*, I. 170: τίς πόθεν εἶς ἀνδρῶν; and Heliand, v. 4974:
     Fragôdun fiundo barn,   *hwilikes he folkes wari:*
     "*Ni bist thu,* etc.,"
where the same abrupt transition from indirect to direct narrative is found.

But phrases such as *mannô folc, heliðo folk* are common in the Heliand.

With the whole passage Collitz (*P.B.B.* XXXVI. 366) compares the meeting of Diomedes and Glaucus in *Iliad* VI. 119 ff.

12. *in chunincriche*, probably to be taken with *ęnan* as above (Braune).

irmindeot, "the whole race of men." *Irmin*- was used as the first element of compounds (cf. AS. *yrmenþeodum* in the Menologium, v. 139, and *eormencynnes* in Beowulf, v. 1957; OS. *irminthiod*, frequently in the Heliand; ON. *jǫrmungrundr*, "the whole earth") originally with the idea of universality (cf. *Translatio S. Alexandri*, c. III.: *Irminsul, quod Latine dicitur universalis columna, quasi sustinens omnia*, though afterwards this idea was often forgotten; cf. Widukind, *Rerum Gestarum Saxonicarum* Lib. I. c. 12: *Hirmin...; quo vocabulo ad laudem vel ad vituperationem usque hodie etiam ignorantes utimur* quoted by Chadwick, *Origin of the English Nation*, pp. 226 ff.

16. *alte anti frote*; cf. Otfrid, II. 12. 24: *altêr inti fruâter*, and Beowulf, v. 2449: *eald ond infrod.*

dat Hiltibrant hætti min fater;   ih heittu Hadubrant.
Forn her ostar giweit,   floh her Otachres nid—
hina miti Theotrihhe   enti sinero degano filu.
20 Her furlaet in lante   luttila sitten
prut in bure   barn unwahsan,
arbeo laosa;   he[r] raet ostar hina.
Det sid Detrihhe   darba gistuontun
fateres mines;   dat uuas so friuntlaos man.
25 Her was Otachre   ummet tirri,
degano dechisto   miti Deotrichhe.
Her was eo folches at ente;   imo was eo fehta ti leop.
Chud was her   chonnem mannum.
Ni waniu ih iu lib habbe...."
30 "†W[et]tu† irmingot" (quad Hildibra*n*t)   "obana
ab heuane,
dat du neo dana halt mit sus sippan man
dinc ni gileitos......."
Want her do ar arme   wuntane bouga
cheisuringu gitan,   so imo se der chuning gap,
35 Huneo truhtin. "Ðat ih dir it nu bi huldi gibu."

---

18. MS. *gihweit.*   22. MS. *herac̄ ostar hina dc̄.*   24. MS. *fatereres.*
After 26 MS. has *darba gistontun,* repeated mechanically from above, v. 23.
30. MS. *W.. tu, Hildibraht.*

18. *floh her Otachres nid*; cf. Beowulf, v. 1200: *searoniðas fleah* (MS. *fealh*) *Eormanrices.*
It is significant that in Hildebrand, the earliest evidence for Dietrich's exile at the Hunnish court, his enemy is Otacher, Odoacer-Odovacar, the Scyrrian or Turcilingian leader of *fœderati*, who in 476 deposed Romulus Augustulus, the last Emperor of the West, and reigned in Italy as Patrician till the invasion of Theodoric (489), by whom he was treacherously slain after the fall of Ravenna (493). In the MHG. epics (Dietrichs Flucht, etc.) Otacher's place is filled by Erminrek; cf. Deor, v. 21 n. An intermediate form of the story is found in the Quedlinburg-Würzburg Chronicles (*MGH. SS.* III. 31, VI. 23) and Ekkehard von Aura (*MGH. SS.* VI. 130 ff.), where Odovacar is the treacherous counsellor of Ermanric, corresponding to the Sibich of later authorities.
20 ff. Perhaps the most satisfactory way of dealing with this much disputed passage (cf. Braune, p. 182) is to take *prut* with v. Grienberger as *pruti* (Gen.), "in his wife's bower." It can then be translated without difficulty as above.
21. *barn unwahsan*; cf. AS. Genesis, v. 2871: *bearn unweaxen.*
23. MS. *dc̄*, which Braune and others regard as dittography for *Det-rihhe*: v. Grienberger compares with the inorganic *þæt* found in certain AS. charters.

by, have told me that my father's name was Hildebrand. I am called Hadubrand. Long ago he departed towards the east: he fled from the hatred of Odovacar, away with Theodoric and many another of his knights. He left behind his hapless son, bereft of his heritage, a little child in his mother's bower. But he rode away to the east. In after years Theodoric had need of my father; he had lost all his friends —he was exceeding wrathful with Odovacar. The most devoted knight by Theodoric's side, he was ever in the forefront of the host: he always loved the fray. He was famous among men of valour; but I deem he is no longer alive."

"I call to witness the Almighty God from heaven above," quoth Hildebrand, "that never hast thou sought the wager of battle with one so near of kin."

And with that he slipped from his arm the twisted rings wrought of imperial gold, which the king, even the lord of the Huns, had bestowed upon him. "This will I give to thee in earnest of good faith."

24. *dat uuas so friuntlaos man*, a figure of speech common in AS. and OS.; cf. Beowulf, v. 11: *þæt wæs god cyning*, etc. It refers to Theodoric rather than to Hildebrand; cf. the prose at the beginning of Guþrúnarkviþa hin forna: *þjóðrekr konungr var með Atla ok hafði þar látit flesta alla menn sina*; Klage, vv. 2061 ff., and Nibelungenlied, str. 2256 ff.
25. *ummet tirri*; cf. Aasen, *Norsk Ordbog*, p. 808ᵇ (Christiania, 1873); *terren* (*tirren*): *hidsig, vred, opirret*, "hot-headed," "angry," "exasperated" (Kögel).
26. *dechisto*, generally taken as the superlative of an adj. corresponding to ON. *þekkr*, "tractable," "obedient." Kögel (*Geschichte der deutschen Litteratur* I. 1. 219) emends to *dehtisto*; cf. OHG. *kideht: devotus*. In any case cf. þiðriks saga, c. 15 (Bertelsen, I. 34):
En sva mikit ann hvar þeirra odrumm ath einguir karlmenn hafa meira vnnazt eptir þvi sem David kongur ok Jonathas.
27. *folches at ente*: cf. AS. Riddle LXXX. 8: *herges at ende*.
30. *W*[et]*tu* (second and third letters illegible in MS.). The twelve different renderings are collected in Braune, p. 183; perhaps the least difficult of these is Grein's *wettu*=OHG. *weizzu*, "ich mache wissen," "rufe zum Zeugen an."
obana ab heuane; cf. Heliand, v. 5799: *oðana fon radure*.
31. *neo dana halt*; cf. Goth. Skeireins, IV. d: *ni þe haldis* (*non idcirco*), and Heliand, v. 2643:
Than hald ni mag thera medun man gimakon fiðan,
though the sense is not quite parallel. If copied correctly it has lost its force here as in the AS., *no þy ær fram meahte* (Beowulf, v. 754).
32. *dinc ni geleitos*; cf. Veldecke's Eneit, v. 77; *teidinc leiden* (v. Grienberger).
33. *wuntane bouga*: cf. Beowulf, vv. 1193, 3134: *wunden gold*; Heliand, v. 554: *wundan gold*.
34. *cheisuringu*, an imperial gold coin; cf. AS. *casering: drachma, didrachma.*

Hadubra*n*t gima[*ha*]lta,   Hiltibra*n*tes sunu:
"Mit geru scal man   geba infahan
ort widar orte.   Du bist dir, alter Hun,
ummet spaher;   spenis mih mit dinem wortun,
40 wili mih dinu speru werpan.
Pist also gialtet man,   so du ewin inwit fuortos.
Ðat sagetun mi   sęolidante
westar ubar Wentilsęo,   dat inan wic furnam.
Tot ist Hiltibrant,   Heribrantes suno."
45 Hiltibra*n*t gimahalta,   Heribra*n*tes suno:

.   .   .   .

"Wela gisihu ih in dinem hrustim,
dat du habes heme   herron goten,
dat du no bi desemo riche   reccheo ni wurti."
"Welaga nu, waltant got (quad Hiltibrant),   wewurt
    skihit.
50 Ih wallota sumaro enti wintro   sehstic ur lante,
dar man mih eo scerita   in folc sceotantero,
so man mir at burc ęnigeru   banun ni gifasta.
Nu scal mih suasat chind   suertu hauwan,
breton mit sinu billiu,   eddo ih imo ti banin werdan.
55 Doh maht du nu aodlihho,   ibu dir din ellen taoc
in sus heremo man   hrusti giwinnan
rauba bi*r*ahanen,   ibu du dar enic reht habes.
Der si doh nu argosto (quad Hiltibrant)   ostarliuto,

---

36. MS. *Hadubraht gimalta.*   45. MS. *Hiltibraht.*
57. MS. *bihrahanen.*

37–8. There is perhaps a parallel to this passage in the Chronicon Novaliciense, III. 22, 23, where Algisus, when offered rings on the point of a spear, refuses to trust himself within reach of it, exclaiming: *Si tu cum lancea ea mihi porrigis, et ego ea cum lancea excipio*; cf. too Egilssaga, c. LV.

39. Cf. Heliand, v. 1376: *spanan mid is spracu.*

41. For the sequence of ideas, cf. þiðriks saga, c. 400 (Bertelsen, II. 338): *hann hæfir sig flutt fram allan sinn aldr med sœmð oc drengskap oc sua er hann gamall orðinn.*

42. Cf. Beowulf, v. 377: *þone sægdon þæt   sæliðende.*

43. *Wentilsęo*, "the Vandal Sea," "Mediterranean," a reminiscence of the days of Gaiseric (428–477), when the Vandal fleet terrorised the Mediterranean; cf. AS. *Wendelsæ* in Elene, v. 231, Alfred's translation of Orosius, etc.

dat inan wic furnam: cf. Beowulf, v. 1080: *wig ealle fornam Finnes þegnas.*

46 ff. Cf. Beowulf, v. 1484 ff.

48. I.e. "You have not lost your lord's favour."

Hadubrand, the son of Hildebrand, replied: "With the spear should one receive a gift, point to point. Thou art of exceeding guile, old Hun. Thou seekest to decoy me with thy words and wilt aim thy spear at me. Thou hast grown old in the practice of treachery. Seafarers who went westwards over the Vandal Sea, have told me that he fell in battle. Dead is Hildebrand, the son of Heribrand."

Then spake Hildebrand, the son of Heribrand.

* * * * *

"By thy garb I see full well that thou hast a generous lord at home; thou art no outcast in this land."

"Woe now is me, Almighty God," quoth Hildebrand. "An evil fate is come upon me. Sixty summers and winters have I wandered in exile from my native land and I was ever stationed in the forefront of the host: yet no man dealt me my deathblow before any stronghold. But now mine own son will smite me with his sword, slay me with his brand, or I must be his slayer. Yet now if thy prowess avail thee, thou canst easily win the harness of so old a man, carry off the spoils, if thou hast any right to them. Now were he the craven of the easterners who

49. *waltant got*: cf. AS. *wealdend god*, OS. *waldand god*.
50. *sehstic*, i.e. 30 summers and 30 winters, a relic of the counting by seasons (*misseri*). It is worth noting that Wolf-Dietrich was likewise in exile for 30 years; cf. Chadwick, *Heroic Age*, p. 155.
In þiðriks saga, c. 396 (Bertelsen, II. 331), the exile lasted 32 years.
51. *sceotantero*, simply "warriors"; cf. Beowulf, v. 1155, etc.
52. *banun ni gifasta*; cf. Elene, v. 477:
  Ne meahton hie swa disige   deað oðfæstan.
53. *suasat*, "own"; cf. AS. *swæs*, and Ásmundarsaga Kappabana, c. IX.:
  Liggr þar inn svási   sonr at höfði.
54. *breton mit sinu billiu*; wk vb, cf. AS. *breodwian* (Müllenhoff). For the phrase, cf. Exodus, v. 199: *billum abreotan*.
  eddo ih imo ti banin werdan; cf. Heliand, v. 644:
  hogda im te banin uuerðon;
and Beowulf, v. 587:
  þeah ðu þinum broðrum   to banan wurde.
55. *ibu dir din ellen taoc*, a common phrase in the poetic diction of the old Teutonic languages; cf. Andreas, v. 460: *gif his ellen deah*, etc.
56. Cf. Waldhere, B 17.
57. *ibu du dar enic reht habes*, either "if you can make good your claim" or "if you have justice on your side."
58. *ostarliuto*, Huns rather than Ostrogoths; cf. Ásmundar saga, where Hildibrandr is styled *Húnakappi*.

der dir nu wiges warne,   nu dih es so wel lustit,
60 gudea gimeinun: niuse de motti,
[*h*]werdar sih hiutu   dero hregilo *r*umen muotti,
erdo desero brunnono   bedero uualtan."
Do lęttun se ærist   asckim scritan,
scarpen scurim,   dat in dem sciltim stont.
65 Do stopu*n* tosamane,   †staimbort† chlu*b*un,
heuwun harmlicco   huittę scilti,
unti im iro lintun   luttilo wurtun,
giwigan miti wabnu*m*.......

61. MS. *werdar sih dero hiutu, hrumen.*   65. MS. *stoptŭ, staim bort*
chludun.

59.   *nu dih es so wel lustit*; cf. Otfrid, i. 1. 14; *so thih es uuola*
lustit.
60.   *gudea gimeinun*; cf. Beowulf, v. 2473: *wroht gemæne.*
niuse de motti; cf. Heliand, v. 224: *he niate ef he môti*; Beowulf, v. 1387:
wyrce se þe mote.
61.   MS. *werdar* for *hwedar* (AS. *hwæðer*).
A parallel to this passage is to be found in þiðriks saga, c. 19 (Bertelsen, i.
19): *og bere sa i brott hvarutveggia er meiri madur er og fræknare verdur þa*
er reynt er (Kögel).
63.   Klaeber, *M. L. N.* xxi. 110 ff., compares Layamon's Brut,
vv. 28322 ff.:
        Summe heo letten ut of scipen
        Scerpe garen scriþen,
and emends *asckim* to *ascki*; but the dat. is not absolutely impossible if
taken in the sense of "let fly with spears."

should refuse thee the combat, the duel, since thy heart is set upon it. Let him find out who can which of us this day is doomed to be stripped of his panoply or to win possession of both these corselets."

Then first they launched their spears, their sharp weapons, so that the shields were pierced. Then they strode together, they clove the......bucklers shrewdly smiting at the white targets until their linden shields, destroyed by the weapons, were of none avail.

64. *scarpen scurim* (for *scurun* perhaps by analogy with *asckim*) in apposition to *asckim*; cf. Heliand, v. 5137:

> *that man ina witnôdi   wâpnes eggiun,*
> *skarpun skurun,*

where *skûr* is generally taken to mean "weapon" (Sievers, *Z.f.d.Ph.* xvi. 113); but cf. Beowulf, v. 1033: *scurheard*, etc.

stont, impersonal, "so that there was a transfixing of the shields."

65. Most editors emend the ms. *stoptun* to *stopun*; cf. Heliand, v. 4875: *stop imu togegnes*, and Rabenschlacht, v. 741 : *zesamane si staphten*.

ms. *staim bort chludun*, regarded by Lachmann as a single compound noun, a kenning for "warriors." It is tempting, however, to emend *chludun* to *chlubun* on the analogy of Maldon, v. 283 : *clufon cellod bord*. The first element of *staimbort* has never been satisfactorily explained. The natural way would be to take it as "stone," hence "jewelled shields"; but I have not seen a single instance of shield-boss set with precious stones from grave-finds of the period, and the only literary evidence, Gregory of Tours' *Historia Francorum*, ix. 28, is not perhaps very valuable, though for later times there is abundant evidence; cf. Nibelungenlied, str. 1640, 2149 ; Egilssaga, c. LXXVIII.

68. Cf. Maldon, v. 228 : *forwegen mid his wæpne*.

GENERAL BIBLIOGRAPHY.

Modern Works.

Brandl, A. Cf. *Pauls Grundriss*(2).

Brooke, Stopford A. *History of Early English Literature to the Accession of King Aelfred*, 2 vols. London, 1892.

—— *English Literature from the Beginning to the Norman Conquest.* London, 1898.

Chadwick, H. M. *Early National Poetry (Camb. Hist. Eng. Lit.* I. 19–40). Cambridge, 1907.

—— *The Origin of the English Nation.* Cambridge, 1907.

—— *The Heroic Age.* Cambridge, 1912.

Clarke, M. G. *Sidelights on Teutonic History in the Migration Period.* Cambridge, 1911.

Grimm, W. K. *Deutsche Heldensage*(3). Gütersloh, 1889.

Gummere, F. B. *Germanic Origins.* New York, 1892.

Heinzel, R. *Über die ostgotische Heldensagen.* Wien, 1889.

Jiriczek, O. L. *Deutsche Heldensagen*, Bd I. Strassburg, 1898.

—— *Northern Hero-Legends* (trans. M. B. Smith). London, 1902.

Ker, W. P. *The Dark Ages.* Edinburgh, 1904.

—— *Epic and Romance*(2). London, 1908.

—— *English Literature; Medieval.* London, 1912.

Kögel, R. *Geschichte der deutschen Litteratur*, I. 1. Strassburg, 1894.

Möller, H. *Das altenglische Volksepos.* Kiel, 1883.

Morley, H. *English Writers*, I.–II.(2) London, 1887–8.

Paul, H. *Grundriss der Germanische Philologie*(1), Bd II. (especially *Heldensage* v. B. Symons; *Gotische Lit.* v. E. Sievers; *Norwegisch-isländische Lit.* v. E. Mogk; *Althoch- u. altniederdeutsche Lit.* v. R. Kögel; *Mhd. Lit.* v. F. Vogt; *Altenglische Lit.* v. B. ten Brink; *Altgermanische Metrik* v. E. Sievers). Strassburg, 1891–3.

—— *Grundriss*(2), Bd III. (especially *Gotische Lit.* v. W. Streitberg; *Ahd. u. and. Lit.* v. R. Kögel u. W. Brückner; *Mhd. Lit.* v. F. Vogt; *Norwegisch-isländische Lit.* v. E. Mogk; *Englische Lit.* v. A. Brandl; *Heldensage* v. B. Symons). Strassburg, 1896–1909.

Stjerna, K. M. *Essays on questions connected with the Old English poem of Beowulf* (Viking Club Series). Coventry, 1912.

ten Brink, B. *Early English Literature.* London, 1883.
—— *Geschichte der englischen Literatur,* hrsg. v. A. Brandl, Bd I.
Strassburg, 1899.
Wülker, R. P. *Grundriss der Geschichte der angelsächsischen Literatur,*
Bd II. Leipzig, 1885.
—— *Geschichte der englischen Literatur.* Leipzig, 1896.
Zeuss, J. C. *Die Deutschen und die Nachbarstämme.* München, 1837
(facsimile reprint, Göttingen, 1904).

Gothic.

Feist, S. *Etymologische Wörterbuch der gotische Sprache.* Halle, 1909.
Streitberg, W. *Die Gotische Bibel.* Heidelberg, 1908–10.
Jantzen, H. *Gotische Sprachdenkmäler*(3) (Samml. Göschen). Leipzig,
1909.
Bernhardt, E. *Die gotische Bibel des Vulfila.* Halle, 1884.
Holder, A. *Jordanis de Origine Actibusque Getarum.* Freiburg i. B. u.
Tübingen, 1882.
Mommsen, Th. *Jordanis Romana et Getica* (*M.G.H. Auctores Antiquis-
simi,* v. 1). Berlin, 1882.
    tr. C. C. Mierow. *The Gothic History of Jordanes.* Princeton,
1915.

Anglo-Saxon.

Bosworth, J.—Toller, T. N. *Anglo-Saxon Dictionary.* Oxford, 1898.
Toller, T. N. *Supplement, A—eorþ.* Oxford, 1908.
Grein, C. W. M. *Sprachschatz der angelsächsischen Dichter:* Neuausgabe
von Holthausen-Kohler. Heidelberg, 1912.
Sweet, H. *Anglo-Saxon Reader*(8). Oxford, 1908.
—— *Second Anglo-Saxon Reader.* Oxford, 1887.
Kluge, F. *Angelsächsisches Lesebuch*(3). Halle, 1902.
    tr. A. S. Cook and C. B. Tinker. *Select Translations from Old
English Poetry.* Boston, 1902.
    —— *Select Translations from Old English Prose.* Boston, 1908.
Grein-Wülker. *Bibliothek der angelsächsischen Poesie*(2), 3 vols. Kassel
and Leipzig, 1881–98.
Sedgefield, W. J. *Beowulf*(2). Manchester, 1913.
Wyatt, A. J. and Chambers, R. W. *Beowulf with the Finnsburg
Fragment.* Cambridge, 1914.
Heyne, M.—Schücking, L. L. *Beowulf*(9). Paderborn, 1910.
Zupitza, J. *Beowulf: Autotypes of the Cotton MS. with transliteration
and notes* (E.E.T.S. 77). London, 1882.
    tr. C. G. Child. *Beowulf and the Finnesburh Fragment.* London,
1904.
        J. R. Clark Hall. *Beowulf and the Finnesburg Fragment*(2).
London, 1911.

88   *General Bibliography*

Thorpe, B. *Codex Exoniensis.* London, 1842.
Gollancz, I. *The Poems of the Exeter Book* (with translations), Vol. I. (E.E.T.S. 102). London, 1892.
Chambers, R. W. *Widsith.* Cambridge, 1912.
Gollancz, I. *Cynewulf's Christ* (with translation). London, 1892.
Cook, A. S. *The Christ of Cynewulf.* Boston, 1900.
Kent, C. W. *Elene(2).* Boston, 1902.
Holthausen, F. *Cynewulf's Elene(2).* Heidelberg, 1910.
Krapp, G. P. *Andreas and the Fates of the Apostles.* Boston, 1906.
Strunk, W. jun. *Juliana.* Boston, 1904.
   tr. C. W. Kent. *The Poems of Cynewulf.* London, 1910.
Tupper, F. *The Riddles of the Exeter Book.* Boston, 1910.
Wyatt, A. J. *Old English Riddles.* Boston, 1913.
Kemble, J. M. *Codex Vercellensis,* 2 vols. London, 1843.
Wülker, R. P. *Codex Vercellensis.* Leipzig, 1894.
Förster, M. *Il Codice Vercellese con Omelie e Poesie in Lingua Anglosassone, riprodotto in fototipia.* Roma, 1913.
Holthausen, F. *Die ältere Genesis.* Heidelberg, 1914.
Klaeber, F. *The Later Genesis and other OE. and OS. texts relating to the Fall of Man.* Heidelberg, 1913.
Blackburn, F. A. *Exodus and Daniel.* Boston, 1907.
Cook, A. S. *The Dream of the Rood.* Oxford, 1905.
—— *Judith.* Boston, 1904.
Sedgefield, W. J. *The Battle of Maldon and Poems from the Anglo-Saxon Chronicle.* Boston, 1904.
Grein, C. W. M. *Bibliothek der ags. Prosa,* Bd I.–VII. Kassel, Göttingen, Hamburg, 1872–1910.
Sweet, H. *The Oldest English Texts* (E.E.T.S. 83). London, 1885.
—— *The Anglo-Saxon Version of Gregory's Pastoral Care* (E.E.T.S. 45, 50). London, 1871–2.
—— *King Alfred's Orosius* (E.E.T.S. 79). London, 1883.
Sedgefield, W. J. *King Alfred's Translation of Boethius.* Oxford, 1899.
—— tr. *King Alfred's Version of the Consolations of Boethius.* Oxford, 1900.
Plummer, C. *Bædae Opera Historica,* 2 vols. Oxford, 1896.
   tr. A. M. Sellar. *Beda: Ecclesiastical History of England(2).* London, 1912.
Earle, J. and Plummer, C. *Two Saxon Chronicles Parallel,* 2 vols. Oxford, 1892–9.
   tr. E. E. C. Gomme. *The Anglo-Saxon Chronicle.* London, 1909.
Herzfeld, G. *OE. Martyrology* (E.E.T.S. 116). London, 1900.
Thorpe, B. *The Homilies of Ælfric* (Ælfric Soc.). London, 1844–6.
Napier, A. S. *Wulfstan.* Berlin, 1883.
—— *OE. Glosses* (Anecdota Oxon.). Oxford, 1900.

Wright, T. and Wülker, R. P. *Anglo-Saxon and Old English Vocabularies.* London, 1884.

Stevenson, J. *Rituale Ecclesiae Dunelmensis* (Surtees Soc. 10). 1839.

—— and Waring, G. *Lindisfarne and Rushworth Gospels* (Surtees Soc. 28, 39, 43, 48). 1854–65.

Cockayne, O. *Leechdoms, Wortcunning and Starcraft of Early England* (Rolls Series), 3 vols. London, 1864–6.

Kemble, J. M. *Codex Diplomaticus Anglo-Saxonici Aevi*, 6 vols. London, 1839–48.

Thorpe, B. *Diplomatarium Anglicum Saxonici Aevi.* London, 1865.

Birch, W. de G. *Cartularium Saxonicum*, 4 vols. London, 1883–93.

German.

Schade, O. *Altdeutsches Wörterbuch* (2). Halle, 1882.

Müllenhoff, K. u. Scherer, W. *Denkmäler deutscher Poesie u. Prosa aus den VIII.–XII. Jahrh.* (3) Berlin, 1892.

Eneccerus, M. *Die ältesten deutschen Sprachdenkmäler in Lichtdrücken.* Frankfurt a. M., 1897.

Braune, W. *Althochdeutsche Lesebuch* (7). Halle, 1911.

Steinmeyer, E. u. Sievers, E. *Die Althochdeutsche Glossen*, Bd IV. Berlin, 1879–98.

Sievers, E. *Tatian, lateinisch und altdeutsch* (2). Paderborn, 1892.

Piper, P. *Die Schriften Notkers und seine Schule*, Bd III. Freiburg, 1882–3.

—— *Otfrieds Evangelienbuch* (2), Bd II. Freiburg, 1882–7.

Heyne, M. *Héliand nebst den Bruchstücken der altsächs. Genesis* (4). Paderborn, 1905.

—— *Kleinere altniederdeutsche Denkmäler* (2). Paderborn, 1877.

Gallée, J. H. *Altsächsische Sprachdenkmäler.* Leiden, 1894.

Lachmann, K. *Der Nibelunge Noth und die Klage* (13). Berlin, 1910.

tr. M. Armour. *The Fall of the Nibelungs* (Everyman). London, 1908.

Martin, E. *Kûdrun.* Halle, 1872.

tr. M. P. Nichols. *Gudrun.* Boston, 1889.

Kinzel, K. *Lamprechts Alexander.* Halle, 1884.

Deutsche Heldenbuch, Bd v. Berlin, 1866–75.

I. Jänicke, O. *Biterolf u. Dietlieb, Laurin u. Walberan* (1866).

II. Martin, E. *Alpharts Tod, Dietrichs Flucht, Rabenslacht* (1866).

III.–IV. Amelung, A. u. Jänicke, O. *Ortnit u. die Wolfdietriche* (1871–5).

V. Zupitza, J. *Dietrichs Abenteuer* (1870).

Scandinavian.

Cleasby, R. and Vigfússon, G. *Old Icelandic Dictionary.* Oxford, 1879.

90 General Bibliography

Egilsson, S. *Lexicon Poëticum antiquae Linguae Septentrionalis.*
Havniae, 1860.
Of the new edition, revised by Finnur Jónsson for the *Konglige Nordiske Oldskriftselskab, A—lymskufljótr* has appeared. København, 1913-.
Fritzner, J. *Ordbog over det gamle norske Sprog*, Bd III. Kristiania, 1886–96.
Die Lieder der älteren Edda(2), hrsg. v. Hildebrand-Gering. Paderborn, 1904.
Sæmundar Edda, F. Jónsson bjó til prentunar. Reykjavík, 1905.
   tr. B. Thorpe. *Edda Sæmundar hinns Fróða*, 2 vols. London, 1866.
   O. Bray. *The Elder or Poetic Edda*, part I. (Viking Club Series). Coventry, 1908.
Corpus Poeticum Boreale, ed. G. Vigfússon and F. York Powell. Oxford, 1883.
Edda Snorra Sturlasonar sumptibus legati Arnamagnæani, t. III. Havniae, 1848–87.
—— F. Jónsson bjó til prentunar. Reykjavík, 1907.
   tr. G. W. Dasent. *The Prose or Younger Edda* (omitting *Skaldskaparmál*). Stockholm, 1842.
   R. B. Anderson. *The Younger Edda.* Chicago, 1880.
Origines Islandicae, ed. Vigfússon and Powell. Oxford, 1905.
Islendinga Sögur búið hefir til prentunar V. Ásmundarson, 37 vols. Reykjavík, 1891–1902.
Altnordische Sagabibliothek, hrsg. v. G. Cederschiöld, H. Gering u. E. Mogk, 13 vols. Halle, 1892-.
   tr. G. W. Dasent. *The Story of Burnt-Njal*, 2 vols. Edinburgh, 1861. (Several times reprinted in one volume.)
   —— *The Story of Gisli the Outlaw.* Edinburgh, 1866.
   E. Head. *The Story of Viga-Glúm.* London, 1866.
   E. Magnússon and W. Morris. *The Story of Grettir the Strong.* London, 1869.
   —— *Three Northern Love Stories.* London, 1875.
   —— *The Saga Library*, vols. I.–II. London, 1891–2.
   G. A. Hight. *The Grettir Saga* (Everyman). London, 1913.
   W. C. Green. *The Story of Egil Skallagrímsson.* London, 1893.
   M. A. C. Press. *The Laxdæla Saga.* London, 1899.
Heimskringla, udgivet af F. Jónsson, 4 vols. København, 1893–1901.
—— udgivet af F. J., 1 vol. København, 1911.
   tr. Morris and Magnússon. *The Saga Library*, vols. III.–VI. London, 1893–1905.
Flateyjarbók, udg. G. Vigfússon og C. R. Unger, 3 vols. København, 1860–8.
   tr. J. Sephton, *The Saga of King Olaf Tryggwason.* London, 1895.
40 *Islendingar* Þættir, Þ. Jónsson gaf út. Reykjavík, 1904.

Fornmanna Sögur, 12 vols. Kjøbenhavn, 1825–37.
Fornaldarsögur Norðrlanda, búið hefir til prentunar V. Ásmundarson, 3 vols. Reykjavík, 1885–9.
  tr. Morris and Magnússon. *Völsunga Saga.* London, 1870.
Skjöldunga Saga, ed. A. Olrik (from *Aarb. f. n. O.* 1894). Kjøbenhavn, 1894.
Saxo Grammaticus. *Historia Danica,* ed. A. Holder. Strassburg, 1885.
  tr. O. Elton. *The First Nine Books of Saxo.* London, 1892.
Þiðriks saga af Bern, ed. H. Bertelsen, 2 vols. København, 1905–11.

INDEX OF NAMES

MENTIONED IN THE POEMS

Wa, Wb = Waldhere A and B.   AS, N, I = Anglo-Saxon, Norwegian and
Icelandic Runic Poems.   F = Finn.   D = Deor.   H = Hildebrand.

Printed in the United States
By Bookmasters